FIRST BOOK

OF

MODERN LACE
KNITTING

BY

MARIANNE KINZEL

DOVER PUBLICATIONS, INC.

NEW YORK

Published in Canada by General Publishing
Company, Ltd., 30 Lesmill Road, Don Mills,
Toronto, Ontario.
Published in the United Kingdom by Constable
and Company, Ltd., 10 Orange Street, London WC 2.

This Dover edition, first published in 1972, is a
corrected republication of the work originally
published in 1954 by Artistic Needlework Publications in England. It also contains a new Preface by
the author.

International Standard Book Number: 0-486-22904-1
Library of Congress Catalog Card Number: 72-86063

Manufactured in the United States of America
Dover Publications, Inc.
180 Varick Street
New York, N. Y. 10014

𝔄 𝔇𝔢𝔡𝔦𝔠𝔞𝔱𝔦𝔬𝔫

TO

ENGLAND

refuge through centuries
of the persecuted, the proscribed, the people without a country,
where my husband and I sought haven in exile
and found most happily
a welcome, a country and a home.

CONTENTS

PREFACE
to the Dover Edition

I am indebted to Dover Publications, Inc., for the republication of this book, which was out of print for many years. It offers me the opportunity to comfort my ever-faithful knitting friends throughout the English-speaking world, of whom so many had written to me asking for my designs. I have no doubt that this new Dover edition will also result in enlarging the circle of knitters, especially in the United States of America, who may thus be encouraged to take up lace knitting as a new venture.

The text in the Dover edition is unabridged and slightly corrected. The Acknowledgments and Postscript which were in the original have been omitted because they are no longer applicable.

M.K.

July, 1972

Author's Introduction

A great number of books have been written about the ART OF KNITTING, its technique, origin, and its development in modern times. Some of these books have taken years of research and give the reader and knitter all the knowledge needed to cultivate and appreciate this old craft, and to master it to perfection.

It is, therefore, not for me to dwell upon such a widely-explored subject but with my designs, presented in this book, I hope to pay a small contribution to the creative world of needlework. I also intend to inspire the needlewoman of to-day to take up, in a new fashion, the old and fascinating art of lace knitting which enjoyed a tremendous popularity in the 18th and 19th centuries. During that period, this craft produced in many European countries, countless samples of rare beauty and attained an exceptionally high standard. The knitter of those days used the finest lace thread and extremely fine needles to achieve open lace patterns, which were worked into garments and accessories. But the use of these wire-like needles made the work very tedious, and it must have taken months, if not years, to complete some of those knitted lace designs we admire to-day as heirlooms or museum pieces. Perhaps because of the laborious work attached to this sort of knitting, and because of the influence of the industrial revolution, which in general resulted in a marked deterioration in the art of creating hand-made lace, lace knitting went out of fashion.

It was during the years between the two world wars that new patterns for lace knitting appeared in some of the continental countries, especially Austria and Germany, and brought the almost forgotten art into vogue again. These designs were based, principally, upon the old technique of medallion knitting, in combination with well-known lace stitches, thus creating completely new samples of outstanding beauty. This revived craft was generally known as " ROUND ART KNITTING," and very large lace cloths of one or even two yards diameter were worked in one piece without any joins. Many needlework and art schools sponsored this re-animated art by including the subject in their syllabus. Soon we were taught how to design flower and leaf-shaped forms suited to the technique of knitting, and their application into lace-stitch background. Materials used were medium-fine linen thread or crochet cotton, but the wire-like needles were replaced by sock needles. Due to the comparatively thick knitting pins, the result was a cobweb-like product which grew rapidly in the hands of a skilled knitter in contrast to the slowness of the old-fashioned craft.

Knitted lace is, of course, not by any means as valuable as a fine pillow lace, a needlerun or a needlepoint lace, the latter being considered the most exquisite of all time. But in these crowded days of our modern age, very few women have the long leisure hours required to learn and practise the noble art of true lace-making. Yet, the modern woman, in spite of her crowded programme, still loves to grace her surroundings with fine needlework, and a luxurious piece of lace in the form of a doily or table cloth, curtain or bedspread, was never surpassed in beauty, and will never fail to lend a festive note to any home.

Knitted lace, although unable to compete in value, can compete in beauty, with the lace of olden times. Examples like gossamer can be produced with a set of knitting needles and fine thread of cotton or linen. Since these designs of modern lace knitting can be worked in a comparatively short time, and at very small cost, the craft lends itself to our modern mode of life, and can be taken up by any needlewoman who is conversant with working from knitting instructions.

The book before you is far from being a complete work on modern lace knitting. It represents only one of the latest developments of this craft, applied to household accessories.

The first chapter of the book deals with the basic instructions which should be studied very carefully. It contains enlargements of common lace stitches used for the various designs, information about the materials required, and directions for starting and finishing the samples with the help of photo-diagrams.

The second chapter consists mostly of designs worked on two needles. The first two are very simple patterns indeed, and could only be referred to as open-work knitting, not lace knitting. They will be useful for knitters who take up this work for the first time, since there is a slight difference between wool and cotton knitting. Very often an adjustment of the tension is needed to obtain a more evenly worked lace fabric. The Rose-leaf design for chair set and curtains, as well as the candle-light pattern designed for the bedspread are typical examples of modern lace knitting.

For the third chapter I created designs which demonstrate the technique of ROUND ART KNITTING worked on four needles. A novice in this kind of knitting should carefully study the easy-to-start method which is explained, with the help of photo-diagrams, in the basic instructions. The small pieces like luncheon set and cheval set, could be worked first to obtain the necessary experience before undertaking the venture of knitting the large dinner cloth Sun Ray. Since, even in the largest designs, certain units of stitches repeat again and again, the knitter will soon find that it is not more difficult to knit round than to work to and fro, as done in patterns knitted on two needles.

The fourth chapter introduces square designs of various sizes. Although the same method of commencement is used for both round and square cloths, square designs are quite differently developed. A regular increase is used to form the four corners, thus giving the lace a perfectly square shape when finished.

May I emphasise that knitting stitches used for the working of all the designs presented in this book are very few and very simple. I do expect that the reader of this book is familiar with the basic knitting stitches we all learn in school. Also the most elementary knowledge of crochet, making a chain and a double crochet, is expected, since many of the lace pieces worked in modern technique are crocheted off, and not cast off, to give the lace a more dainty finish. No more knowledge is needed and therefore, it should be possible for any average knitter to follow, without difficulties, the directions of all the patterns compiled. Fully written instructions, as well as charts, are given for every article photographed, and the additional Adaptation of Pattern will enable the knitter to work many more useful and decorative household accessories.

And now a final word! I myself have spent many enjoyable hours in making lace; as a child, knitting my first doily under my mother's guidance; as a student in the Art and Needlework College in Prague, making my first experiments in original designs; and later as a teacher in Czechoslovakia and in England, trying to impart to my pupils my own joy in this beautiful craft. Now, to you my readers, may I wish that same pleasure in creating and the same pride in possessing treasured examples of this most delightful and rewarding of crafts—Modern Lace Knitting.

CHAPTER I

BASIC INSTRUCTIONS

Abbreviations used in Working Instructions

The abbreviations adopted in the working instructions of the designs are such as are most generally used in knitting patterns and will be familiar to any knitter.

K. = Knit.

K.1 = Knit 1 stitch.

P. = Purl.

P.1 = Purl 1 stitch.

K.1B. = Knit 1 stitch through the back.

Sl.1 = Slip 1 stitch from the left needle to the right-hand needle without knitting it.

Psso. = Pass the slip stitch over.

Yo. = Yarn over i.e. bring the yarn forward between the needles and take it back over the right-hand needle ready for the next stitch. (In wool patterns this action is usually described as ' wool forward.')

Yo.2 = Yarn over twice.

K.2 tog. = Knit 2 stitches together.

Sl.1, K.1, psso. = Slip 1 stitch, knit 1 stitch and pass the slipped stitch over.

Sl.1, K.2 tog., psso. = Slip 1 stitch, knit 2 stitches together, pass slipped stitch over.

Sl.2, K.2 tog., p2sso. = Slip 2 stitches, knit 2 stitches together, pass 2 slipped stitches over.

M.2 = Make 2 stitches into next stitch, i.e. Knit 1 stitch and Purl 1 stitch into the same stitch before slipping it off the needle.

M.3 = Make 3 stitches into next stitch, i.e. Knit 1, Purl 1, K.1 into the front of the same stitch before slipping it off the needle.

M.5 = Make 5 stitches into Yarn over of previous round, i.e., Knit 1 (Purl 1, Knit 1) twice into Yo. of previous round before slipping it off the needle.

M.6 = Make 6 stitches into double Yarn over of previous round, i.e. (Knit 1, Purl 1) 3 times into Yo. 2 of previous round before slipping it off the needle.

(K.1 o.1) = Knit 1 stitch over the second, i.e. take the needle behind the first stitch and insert knitwise into the second stitch. Knit this second stitch and leave it on the left needle, and then knit the first stitch. Now slip both stitches off the needle. The final effect is that the first stitch crosses over the second.

st. = Stitch.

sts. = Stitches.

ch. = Chain.

d.c. = Double crochet.

rep. = Repeat.

incl. = Inclusive.

X = This sign in front of a round means : Knit first stitch of round from first needle on to the third needle. Slip first stitch from second needle on to first needle, and then slip first stitch from third needle on to the second needle. Now proceed to knit the marked pattern round.

When using a circular pin knit the first stitch of round plain, adding it to the previous round, and then start to knit the marked pattern round.

XX = Do as explained above with 2 stitches.

* = Asterisk : Repeat the instructions between the asterisks as many times as stated.

( ) = Brackets : Knit the instructions inside the brackets as many times as specified after closing bracket.

Materials

CROCHET COTTON—LINEN THREAD

It is important to choose yarns of first-class quality for lace knitting, since most of the designs are worked in very open lace stitches, and are more liable to wear and tear than a closely knitted fabric.

The originals photographed throughout the book are worked in white or light écru crochet cotton, of the number specified in the working instructions. Fine linen thread of equal thickness is just as suitable, and may even stress the lacy character of the work, but it is not perhaps, as easy to obtain as mercerized or plain crochet cotton. Do not use silks, rayon, or any other yarn with a highly polished surface, or of conspicuous colour, as this is not in the lace-making tradition.

For a beginner in lace knitting, it may be advisable to take a slightly thicker thread than stated in the working instructions of the chosen design. This depends on the skill of the knitter and her ability to adjust her tension to cotton knitting.

KNITTING NEEDLES—CIRCULAR PIN

Knitting pins and knitting needles required for lace knitting are the usual kind, available in every needlework shop. A rustless, lightweight, metal needle, coated with a fine grey film, assures smooth working. Uncoated steel or aluminium needles should not be used since they incline to blacken the fabric. The size of knitting pin or needles is always given in the working instructions of the designs concerned and are usually either No. 12 or No. 13.

For lace pieces worked on two needles, use the ordinary knitting pins with knob-ends, to prevent the stitches from slipping off.

For working round and square designs, as in Chapter III and IV, four double-pointed knitting needles (sock needles) are needed for the start. Smaller designs like luncheon mats etc. are completed on four needles. The method in each case is the same as the working of a sock, having the stitches on three needles and knitting with the fourth.

When working one of the larger lace pieces it is impossible to manage with double-pointed knitting needles when the design has grown to a certain size. It is therefore absolutely essential to continue and finish the work with a circular knitting needle. The most usual kinds on the market are the plated steel circular pin and the nylon circular pin. Both are suited for working with fine threads and the choice is left to the knitter. I, personally, prefer the nylon circular pin since it is light and flexible, and so designed to allow the pin to be held normally as when working with two pins.

Knitters are often rather reluctant to use the circular needle, but having once experimented with this more unusual knitting implement they find it most pleasing to work with. It is, of course, the ideal tool for round knitting.

Circular knitting needles are available in various lengths, measured from point to point, and in all the sizes needed for our purpose. The length of the circular needle selected depends on the size of the design to be worked. In general a circular pin of 16 ins. or 24 ins. length is useful to finish a smaller design. A circular pin of 30 ins., 36 ins., or 42 ins., length is essential to complete a large cloth.

The following scale indicates when the stitches could be transferred from the double pointed knitting needle to a circular pin.

From about round 30—16 ins. length circular pin.

From about round 45—24 ins. length circular pin.

From about round 75—30 ins. or 36 ins., circular pin.

From about round 95—42 ins. length circular pin.

It is better to transfer the stitches on to a circular needle when knitting a plain round, and of course, it is stated in the working instructions of each individual design which pin will serve to finish the particular article.

Referring to the size or number of these pins, it should be emphasized that the thickness of the circular needle must be the same as that of the double-pointed needles used for the commencement of the same cloth, for a different size circular pin would alter the gauge of the stitches.

The circular pin not only facilitates round knitting in general, but it also helps less experienced knitters to avoid the formation of uneven loose stitches between the needles.

CROCHET HOOK

Crochet hooks needed for the crocheting-off (more precisely explained in FINISHING OF LACE) are the kind of steel hooks obtainable in all needlework stores. No. 4, 4½, or 5 will serve for the finishing of any of the given household accessories.

FOR AMERICAN KNITTERS

Needle gage British size No. 12 is equivalent to the American size 11 in double pointed steel needles, and size 2 in American circular knitting needles.

British size No. 13 is equivalent to U.S.A. size 12 in double pointed needles, and size 1 in circular needles.

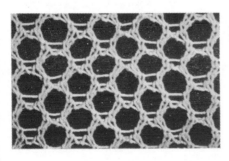

Fig. 1

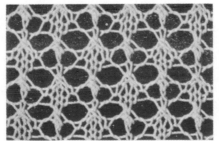

Fig. 2

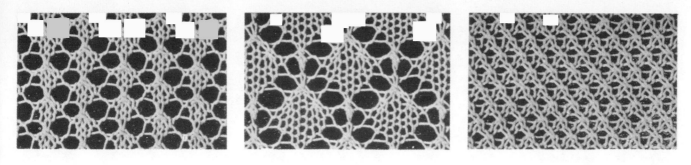

Fig. 3

Lace Stitches

There are lace stitches in existence which are known in every country where women practise the craft of knitting, and it is impossible to trace the time and place of origin of these old lace patterns. The knitters of the Shetland Isles used them in certain combinations for their beautiful, world-famous Shetland Shawls. The needlewomen of the continental countries apply them, in variations, to lace-knitted accessories.

Some of the most common of these stitches were used as ground or filling stitches in the designs collected in this book. The photo-diagrams Fig. 1 to Fig. 7, show enlargements of these simple lace patterns and may help to give the knitter a clearer picture of the formation of stitches when working the designs concerned.

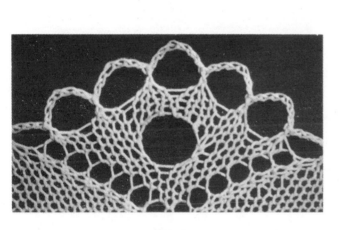

Fig. 4

Fig. 1.   *Daisy Stitch*.
Used as ground-stitch in the curtain-design.

Fig. 2.   *Diamond Stitch*.
Used as ground-stitch for the bedspread-design.

Fig. 3.   *Cross Stitch*.
Used as filling-stitch for the bedspread-design.

Fig. 4.   *Peacock's Eye*.
Used in scallopped edge of Coronet design.

Fig. 5.   *Honeycomb Stitch*.
Used in Coronet-design as filling-stitch.

Fig. 6.   *Ladybird Stitch*.
This is one of the most popular lace stitches, giving a very delicate ground pattern, and was used, as such, for most of the larger designs in the third and fourth chapter.

Fig. 7.   *Ladder Stitch*.
Used in Sun Ray design as filling stitch.

Fig. 5

Fig. 6

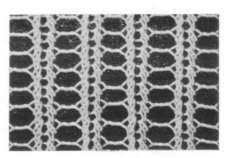

Fig. 7

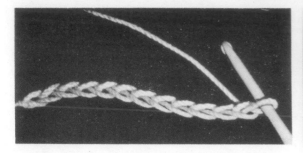

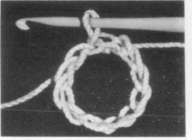

Fig. 8   Fig. 9   Fig. 10

Knitting on Four Needles

The following directions apply in general to the working of all round or square designs compiled in Chapter III and IV of this book.

CASTING-ON

Commence from the centre of the cloth by casting on the number of stitches stated in the working instructions of the chosen design. Divide the stitches on to three needles as suggested and arrange them to form a circle, as when working a sock. Then always knit one round into the back of all stitches (to tighten the cast-on stitches) before following further instructions of the design concerned.

The little hole left in the centre should be drawn together afterwards, when the lace cloth is finished. It is best to thread the long cast-on end, left for this purpose, into a sewing needle and work one over-casting stitch into each cast-on stitch all round the little hole, so drawing it together, and securing the thread at the same time, safely and invisibly.

EASY-TO-START METHOD

The Easy-to-start method, using a crochet hook, presents an alternative means of starting a round or square design, and is an ideal way for beginners in the technique of round knitting, to overcome the difficulty of holding so few stitches on the needles.

The photo-diagrams Fig. 8 to Fig. 16 show the commencement of a design which requires 12 stitches for the start but the same method can be applied to any round or square design using the number of stitches required for the particular pattern.

Fig. 8   Commence by working the same number of chain as cast-on stitches stated in the working instructions of the design (i.e. cast-on 8 stitches—make 8 chain, cast on 10 stitches—make 10 chain etc.).

Fig. 9   Join to a ring by making a slip stitch through the first chain, thus forming at the same time the first stitch.

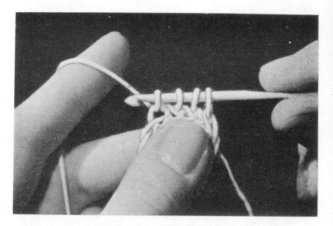

Fig. 11

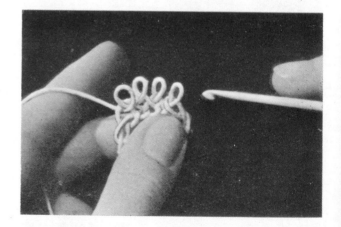

Fig. 12

Fig. 10   Now draw one slip stitch after another through the following three chain

Fig. 11   until you have all four stitches on the crochet hook, thus the first four cast-on stitches are taken up.

Fig. 12   Keep the little ring with the four stitches well in position with your left-hand thumb and middle finger and pull out the crochet hook.

Fig. 13   Then slip into its place the first knitting needle, and pull the thread tight. It is also advisable to push little pieces of cork on to the points of the needle to prevent it from slipping out of the work.

Fig. 14   Draw another four slip stitches with the crochet hook through the next four chain.

Fig. 15   Transfer them again as explained before on to the second needle, and safeguard the stitches from slipping off by putting pieces of cork again on to the ends of the needle.

Fig. 16   Then do the same with the remaining stitches and slip them on to the third needle.

If there are still some difficulties, then I would advise one or two attempts with thicker needles and thicker thread or wool, before starting with the cotton and needles required to work the design. Bone needles may also facilitate the casting-on, since they do not slip so easily out of the work as metal needles. Five-inch-length knitting needles, as used for glove knitting, may also make the beginning process much easier for those knitters who find this a problem.

Having taken up all stitches, knit one or two rounds plain, as usually stated in the working instructions, before knitting the first pattern round of the selected design. The knitter will find through experience that the pieces of cork which prevent the needles from slipping out of the work can be dispensed with after a few rounds of knitting.

The firm little ring which has been so useful in holding in position the small number of starting stitches, can be drawn together afterwards, in the same manner as explained before, i.e. making one cast over stitch into each chain.

GENERAL RULES

When an article is being worked on four needles, the front of the fabric always faces the knitter. Never turn your work when knitting round.

Only pattern rounds are given in the written instructions, (as well as on the charts) and they are marked with numbers. Every round of which the number is missing is knitted plain. In general you will observe that every alternative round is usually a plain round, and if not, special attention is drawn to this fact in the working instructions of the pattern. Nevertheless, the knitter should carefully watch the numbers of the rounds and not adopt the habit, so easily acquired by good knitters, of knitting on, automatically, one pattern and one plain round.

Special attention should be paid if, in a pattern round, a 'yarn over' occurs twice in succession, since in the following plain round, the first corresponding stitch must be knitted, and the second stitch purled or vice versa. Knitters with a slack tension may work only one 'yarn over' in place of the 'double yarn over' stated in the pattern, but great care must be taken that in the following plain round, two stitches are worked into its place as explained above.

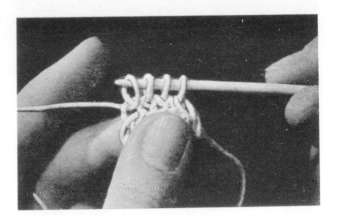

Fig. 13

Fig. 14

Fig. 15

Fig. 16

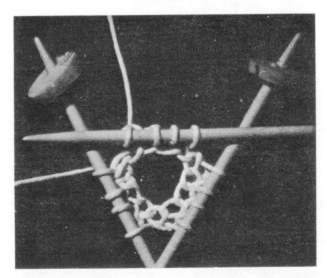

Knitting on Two Pins

CASTING-ON

Designs worked on two knitting pins require usually a greater number of stitches for the start. The method used to obtain these stitches, either by casting-on or by knitting-on, is not important and can be left to the skill of the knitter, since it will not influence the general appearance of the design. If for some reason in a particular pattern, it is preferable to adopt either method, then it will be specially emphasized, as for instance, in the working instructions of the curtains.

GENERAL RULES

When an article is being worked on two pins, the front and the back of the fabric alternately faces the knitter. The front of the lace fabric is composed of pattern rows which are given in the written working instructions (as well as on the charts) and are marked with numbers. All rows of which the numbers are missing are back rows and knitted purl, thus making up the wrong side of the fabric.

Pay **special attention** if, in a pattern row, a **'yarn over'** occurs twice in succession since in the following purl row the first corresponding stitch must be purled and the second stitch knitted. Knitters with slack tension should work only one 'yarn over' where this 'double yarn over' is given in the pattern, but great care must be taken that in the following purl row, two stitches are worked into its place, as explained above.

Tips on Technique

ADJUSTMENT OF TENSION

A knitter used to wool knitting will find that a slight adjustment of tension is needed when taking up lace knitting. Fine threads usually require a tightening of tension but not to such an extent that the stitches will not move upon the needle. Neither should the needles be able to slip out of the work on their own.

In general, tension is something personal which cannot be forced, but watched and adjusted through experience. Therefore, beginners in lace knitting are advised to knit first one or two articles in a thicker cotton to get the feel of the thread, before knitting with the finer yarn recommended in the pattern. Articles, worked in slightly thicker cotton, will be less delicate but otherwise, the general shape of the design will not be disturbed.

Very slack or very tight knitters can also control their tension, by taking either finer or thicker needles than those recommended in the instructions. However, it must be borne in mind that needles which are too fine will not make the fabric appear lacier but closer and more com-pact, unless, of course, a much finer thread is used at the same time. On the other hand, needles which are too thick may widen the gauge of the stitches to such an extent that the design loses its shape.

A change over from needles No. 12 to needles No. 13, or vice versa, should be adequate to adjust the tension if it cannot be done by deliberate control.

Special care must be taken when working with a circular pin that the thread is not tensioned too tightly, otherwise the knitter will have difficulty in pushing the stitches over the join of the pin. Furthermore, it will cause unnecessary strain at the point where the flexible part of the circular needle is connected with the stiff pin-end.

MARKING OF CAST-ON STITCHES

Some of the designs, which are worked on two needles like the curtain and the bedspread, need a fair number of stitches right from the start. To facilitate the counting and checking of the stitches, when commencing it is advisable to slip little loops of coloured thread on to the knitting pin after a certain number of cast-on stitches, (say 30 or 50), thus dividing the cast-on row into equal sections of stitches which can easily be re-counted. See Fig. 17.

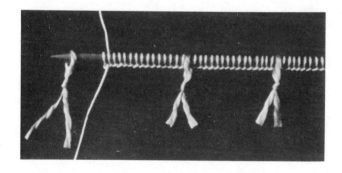

Fig. 17

MARKING OF SECTIONAL UNITS

A beginner in lace knitting may find it helpful to adopt the above system of marking in general, by slipping a coloured loop over the knitting needle after each pattern-unit. These are referred to in the working instructions as sections from [to] or sections from * to *.

MARKING OF THE ROUND

In circular knitting, it is most essential that the beginning of the round is marked very clearly. When knitting with four double-pointed knitting needles, draw in a coloured thread between the first and the last needle when the round is completed. When working with a circular pin mark your round again with a coloured loop, slipping it over the right-hand point of the needle before knitting the first stitch. See Fig. 18. This coloured thread will quite automatically move, with the stitches, all round the circular needle, since it keeps its position all the time between the last and first stitch. As the knitter finishes the round, the loop only needs to be lifted from the left-hand needle-point on to the right-hand point before the first stitch of the next round is knitted.

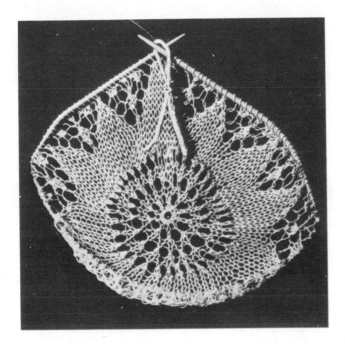

Fig. 18

PICKING UP STITCHES

When knitting lace patterns, it is wise to keep a crochet hook at hand for picking up any stitches you may drop. In case of a more serious accident, for instance, if for some reason a number of stitches slip off the needles, then it is best to put down the work, prepare some thick starch, and wet the area, where the stitches run, carefully with the starch. Place the knitting on a clean towel, wait until it is completely dry, and then pick up the stitches with a crochet hook according to the pattern. The knitter will find that the starch prevents the stitches from running further into the open lace fabric. In this manner, the damage is easily repaired.

JOINING THREADS

Every knitter is familiar with the correct way of joining wool yarns by splicing. This method, however, is useless when knitting with the fine cotton or linen thread recommended in the working instructions of the various designs. The expert knitter, of course, can join the cotton by weaving in the ends, as done in colour knitting. The average knitter may care to try the unorthodox but simple, safe method of joining the fine threads with a reef-knot.

Join the cotton with a reef-knot, leaving ends of 3 or 4 ins. hanging until the article is finished. Then darn in the ends separately and most carefully on the wrong side of the fabric and cut them off when the lace is washed, stretched and ironed.

An alternative method is shown in Fig. 19 and Fig. 20. Make a reef-knot, and when approaching the join, knit with the double threads two stitches before and two stitches after the knot. Then leave two ends of about 2 ins. length hanging on the wrong side of the fabric, and do not cut off, before the lace is washed, stretched and ironed.

When working a design on two needles, join the yarns at the beginning or end of a row. In round knitting it is best done in a plain round, but not in a plain knitted solid part like the middle of a leaf, but rather in the open, lacy fabric of the design where it cannot be noticed so easily.

Those unable to make a reef-knot may use an ordinary knot, and although it is not quite correct, it will serve its purpose, if the ends of the yarn are worked in, as explained above. Never join threads with just a reef-knot or knot and cut off the ends, nor trust a knot you may find in the middle of a ball of cotton.

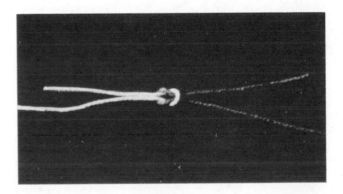

Fig. 19

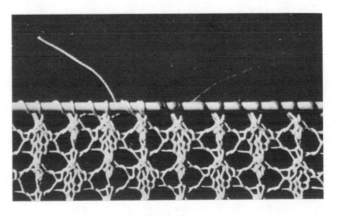

Fig. 20

21

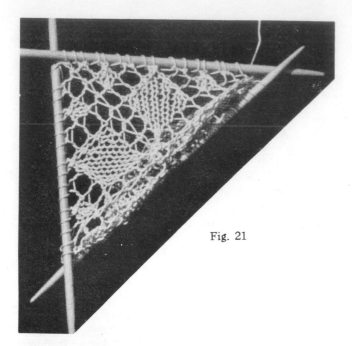

Fig. 21

WORKING OF SQUARE DESIGNS

This is just a special hint and it can be completely ignored should the knitter find the idea rather too foreign. It refers to the working of square designs, as presented in the fourth chapter of the book.

When starting a square design the cast-on stitches rae divided in such a manner that one side of the square is worked on the first needle, one side on the second needle, and two sides on the third needle, since there are four sides to the square. As it takes quite a number of rounds before a circular needle can be used, the knitter may find

Fig. 22

that the stitches forming the corners tend to pull apart, especially on both sides of the third needle. (Fig. 21.) To avoid this irregularity, the stitches on the third needle can be equally divided by using an additional needle. Thus we have the stitches for each quarter separately, on one needle, and knit with the fifth. (Fig. 22.)

It is not wise to have the small number of cast-on stitches already on four needles. Therefore, work first according to instructions of the designs concerned up to round 10 or 15, and then the fifth needle can be used as explained above. If the knitter does not find it convenient to use this extra needle, then carry on with four needles until a circular pin can be used.

Finishing of Lace

CASTING-OFF

Many of the household accessories in Chapter II require, when knitted, only a simple cast-off row as finish.

Any method familiar to the knitter can be used, whether it is casting-off with a hook, binding-off or the so-called suspended casting-off, providing it is worked to the same tension as the knitting and that great care is taken that the selvedge formed by the casting-off stretches to the proper measurements. To strengthen the selvedge edges all round, a row of double crochet is often recommended but this is fully explained in the working instructions of the respective article.

CROCHETING-OFF

In Modern Lace Knitting, crocheting-off was adopted as a new method to give the lace pieces a more dainty finish. It achieves the most effective results when used for designs worked in round knitting, as presented in Chapters III and IV, but is also a perfect finish for the scalloped curtains and chair set.

This very simple way of securing the stitches does not require an expert knowledge of crochet, but only the working of chain and double crochet is needed to follow the instructions.

After knitting the last purl row of a design worked on two pins, or last plain round of lace worked on four needles or a circular pin, we do not cast-off at all but start to finish the edge immediately, with a chain of crochet. Three, four, or even five stitches are crocheted together in a group with one double crochet and a certain number of chain are made to link those groups of stitches, working all along the row or round of the lace.

The number of stitches taken together and the number of chain made to form the little loops, between the groups of stitches, vary and depend on the individual designs, as seen in the working instructions. The chain edge has not to contract the outer edge of the lace but must allow for the stretching into a scallop etc. .A needlewoman used to very tight crochet work may therefore be advised to work, perhaps, one or two more chain than stated in the instructions concerned.

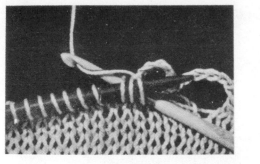

Fig. 23

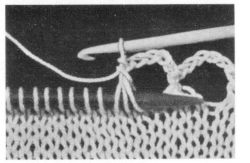

Fig. 24

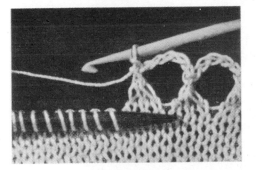

Fig. 25

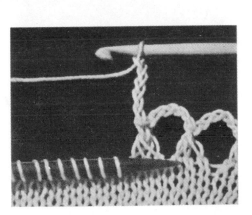

Fig. 26

Fig. 23　Insert crochet hook into the back of the number of stitches to be taken together into one group by one double crochet.

Fig. 24　Make sure you finish the double crochet while the stitches are still on the needle.

Fig. 25　Now take the stitches, which were crocheted together, off the needle.

Fig. 26　Then work required number of chain.
Work all round, repeating the action from Fig. 23 to Fig. 26, until all stitches are crocheted off the pin or needles. Join the last chain with a slip stitch on to first double crochet, break off the thread and secure invisibly.

Fig. 27　Shows the work in progress.

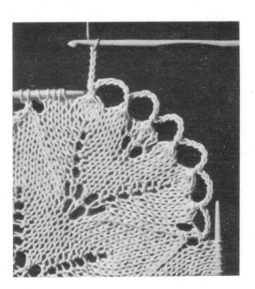

Fig. 27

Photo-diagrams Fig. 23 to Fig. 26 should help to make this method fully understood. The diagram Fig. 27 shows the crocheting-off on a doily, worked with a circular pin, but it is the same method if applied to the finishing of lace worked on two pins.

Washing and Stretching

Just as the parts of a woollen jumper or frock should be blocked out before being stitched together, to give the finishing touch to a woollen garment, knitted lace, too, needs some special treatment to give it a perfect finish. After all, if we spend so many hours knitting a garment, or as demonstrated in this book, knitting a piece of lace, why not spend one or two hours more to complete the article in a proper and expert way? The crisp, lacy look results from the final treatment which can be achieved with hardly any cost.

WASHING

Wash the finished article in a warm lather of mild soap powder or soap flakes.

Do not rub hard but squeeze the lace gently and rinse well in lukewarm water before it is steeped into the prepared starch.

STARCHING

We are, of course, all aware that ordinary starch is not used when treating lace, nor would I advise it, should the article concerned be a precious bobbin or a needlepoint lace. Since the designs presented in this book are not meant to be heirlooms, shut away in a glass case, but household accessories to be used every day, starch will not harm the thread, and knitted lace needs this extra strengthening to retain a perfect shape for a longer time. The designs photographed are slightly stiffened with the warm water starch commonly used for table linen etc. For small doilies, for instance, luncheon mats, a thicker solution of starch is recommended to keep them clean and crisp longer. A satisfactory method is to take one table-spoonful of starch to one pint of water. For larger cloths which should drape well, two or three spoonfuls of starch are sufficient to six pints of water. When the lace is washed, rinsed and starched, do not dry but leave it wet for stretching.

STRETCHING

The working instructions of all the designs give accurate measurements to prepare the paper patterns which should be used for the pinning-out of the lace. Take white or brown paper which does not leave any colour when wet. Place the paper pattern on to a thick card board, card table, piece of felt or perhaps the wrong side of your hearth rug, in short, anything that will allow for an easy insertion of pins. For a very large cloth, the carpet may have to be used. Make sure to have rustless pins for the process of pinning out.

The photo-diagrams below, Fig. 28 to Fig. 33, demonstrate, with the help of doily ' Coronet ', the method of stretching a round cloth from start to finish. Since the method of pinning out is in principle the same, whether

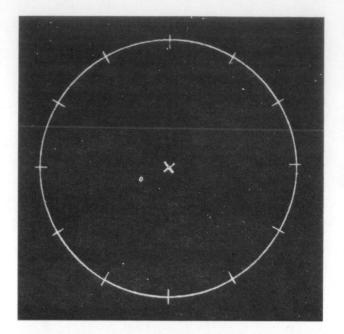

Fig. 29

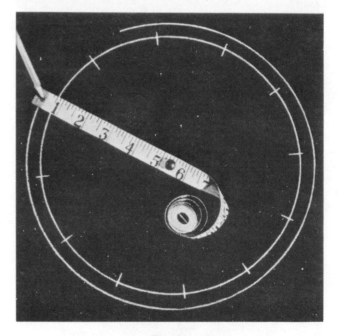

Fig. 30

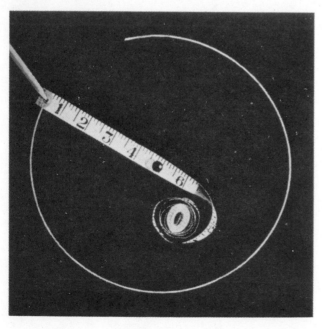

Fig. 28

it is a large or a small cloth, a square or a round one, the photo-diagrams together with the working instructions of the individual designs should give a clear picture of the process.

Fig. 28 Take a tape measure and fasten it down with a pin in the middle of your paper, at the point which is half the diameter of the circle you require to draw.

Insert the pencil into the eyelet hole of the tape measure and draw a circle, keeping the pin in position and the tape measure well stretched.

Fig. 29 Set the marks round the circle, needed for the inner points of the scallops, their distance being always stated in the working instructions,

Fig. 30 Now draw a second outer circle which gives the right size of the cloth.

Fig. 31 Take the washed, rinsed and starched cloth, and pin down the middle of the cloth on to the centre of your circle. Then fasten, with one pin only, the two loops of chain on to the marks of the inner circle. These are the inner points of the scallop. It is advisable to pin down the points opposite to each other in turn.

Fig. 32 Proceed with pinning down on to the outer circle, half way along the space left for each scallop, the loops of chain which form the outer points of the scallops.

Fig. 33 Place the remaining loops of chain into position, thus trying to shape the scallops according to photo.

IRONING

Leave the lace cloth pinned-out, till completely dry. Then remove pins and press carefully, without pulling, to give the thread the final smooth finish. A clean, dry cloth may be placed on to the lace before applying the iron.

Fig. 32

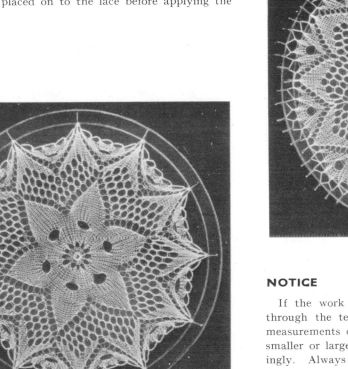

Fig. 31

Fig. 33

NOTICE

If the work does not stretch to the suggested size, through the tension being too slack or too tight, the measurements can easily be altered by making either a smaller or larger circle and adjusting the marks accordingly. Always stretch to capacity.

A perfect appearance of knitted lace can only be achieved by stretching the article after each washing. For that reason keep the sheet of paper, on which the lace was pinned out the first time, for later use.

Chart Instructions in English

Charts are given as an alternative to written instructions, for knitters who may find it rather trying to follow the long lines of printed directions.

The chart signs are evolved by the designer in such a way that they symbolize, in their form, the stitch or action they represent, thus giving, already the outline of the pattern side of the finished lace fabric. A knitter used to chart reading can see at a glance how a pattern is developed, a fact which eliminates the endless counting of stitches and reduces the possibilities of errors. Once familiar with the symbols which, being so few, can be memorized easily, the knitter will be amazed to find how much more quickly she can work from a chart than from written instructions.

It is, of course, left to the reader to decide which method of following a pattern she prefers, but the chart is quite indispensable for those who may one day try their skill as designers of new patterns.

GENERAL RULES FOR CHART READERS

Every line on the chart is read from right to left as the knitting of a row, or round, proceeds in the same direction, each needle being knitted from the right to the left, too.

Empty squares on the chart have no meaning but are necessary to give a clear picture of the pattern, also to simplify the reading of the chart.

For designs worked on two needles, every chart line signifies a section of the front or pattern row, and is marked with a number. All rows of which the numbers are missing are back rows and worked purl.

For designs knitted on four needles or a circular pin, every chart line presents a section of one pattern round and is marked with a number. Every round of which the number is missing, knit plain.

Where part of a chart line is embraced by a bracket, the number of repetitions of this section is given below the chart. Chart lines marked by a double arrow are also repeated, as stated in the relevant instructions.

Whenever in doubt compare with the fully written working instructions of the pattern concerned. The knitter is, of course, expected to have read first the BASIC INSTRUCTIONS in Chapter I of this book.

The casting-on and the finishing of a design should always be taken from the written directions.

KEY FOR CHART

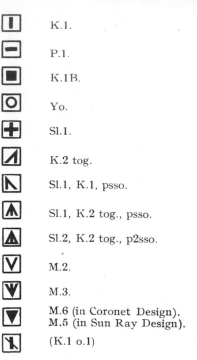

K.1.

P.1.

K.1B.

Yo.

Sl.1.

K.2 tog.

Sl.1, K.1, psso.

Sl.1, K.2 tog., psso.

Sl.2, K.2 tog., p2sso.

M.2.

M.3.

M.6 (in Coronet Design).
M.5 (in Sun Ray Design).

(K.1 o.1)

NOTICE

If a Yo. occurs twice in succession the first corresponding stitch in the following row or round is knitted, the second stitch purled unless otherwise stated in the pattern.

X   This sign in front of a chart line means: Knit first stitch of the round plain, adding the same to the previous round. Then proceed by knitting the marked pattern round.

X X   Do as explained above but move two stitches instead of one.

⌐   The bracket on top of the last chart line indicates the number of stitches taken together by one double crochet.

The figures stand for the number of chain combining these groups of stitches.

Chart Instructions in French
Explications Françaises des Cartes

Vous lisez chaque rang de la carte de droite à gauche, c'est à dire dans le même sens que vous travaillez. Les carreaux vides de la carte n'ont aucune signification, mais ils simplifient la lecture de la carte.

Pour les modèles exécutés sur deux aiguilles, chaque rang de la carte représente une partie d'un rang du motif (c'est à dire de l'endroit du travail), et il est marqué d'un numéro. Tous les rangs dont les numéros manquent sont des rangs de l'envers du travail et sont tricotés à l'envers.

Pour les modèles exécutés sur quatre aiguilles (à deux pointes) ou sur une aiguille circulaire, chaque rang de la carte représente une partie d'un rang du motif et il est marqué d'un numéro ; chaque rang dont le numéro manque est tricoté à l'endroit.

Lorsqu'une partie d'un rang de la carte est mise entre crochets le chiffre au-dessous des crochets indique combien de fois il faut répéter cette partie. Le chiffre qui se trouve à côté de, ou au-dessous d'un rang de la carte marqué de deux flèches, indique combien de fois il faut répéter ce rang.

X Ce symbole devant un rang de la carte signifie : tricoter à l'endroit la première maille du rang et ajouter cette maille au rang précédent. Puis continuer en tricotant le rang marqué.

X X Suivre les explications comme ci-dessus, mais ajouter deux mailles, au lieu d'une maille, au rang précédent.

⌒ Ce symbole indique combien de mailles il faut prendre ensemble pour faire un double-crochet.

5, 7 etc. ceci indique combien de points de chaînette il faut faire entre les groupes de mailles qui sont prises ensemble pour faire un double-crochet.

Knit plain (knit)—Tricoter à l'endroit.

Purl—Tricoter à l'envers.

Stitch (stitches)—Maille (mailles).

Chain—Point de chaînette.

Double-Crochet — Double-Crochet.

Row—Rang.

Round—Tour.

Repeat—Répéter.

Times—Fois.

Part—Partie.

Casting-on—Monter les mailles.

Finishing—Rabattre les mailles.

Stretching—Tension du travail fini.

▯	Une maille à l'endroit.
▭	Une maille à l'envers.
▮	Une maille à l'endroit prise par derrière.
⊙	Passer la laine devant le travail : c'est à dire, faire un jeté simple.

Quelquefois vous faites deux jetés de suite : au rang suivant vous tricotez le premier jeté à l'endroit, le deuxième à l'envers.

✚	Une maille glissée en la prenant à l'endroit.
◿	Deux mailles ensemble à l'endroit.
◺	Un surjet simple, c'est à dire, glisser une maille, une maille à l'endroit, rabattre la maille glissée.
⩑	Une maille glissée, deux mailles ensemble à l'endroit, rabattre la maille glissée.
⩕	Deux mailles glisées, deux mailles ensemble à l'endroit, rabattre les mailles glisées.
⩒	Faire une augmentation, c'est à dire tricoter une maille à l'endroit, une maille à l'envers dans la même maille.
⩔	Faire deux augmentations, c'est à dire tricoter une maille à l'endroit, une maille à l'envers, puis une deuxième maille à l'endroit dans la même maille.
▼	Faire cinq augmentations, c'est à dire dans le premier jeté (du jeté double) du rang précédent faire une maille à l'endroit, une maille à l'envers, une maille à l'endroit. Dans le deuxième jeté du jeté double du rang précédent faire une maille à l'envers, une maille à l'endroit, une maille à l'envers (Coronet Design). Faire quatre augmentations (Sun Ray Design).
◣	Tricoter une maille à l'endroit au-dessus de la maille suivante : c'est à dire : Mettre l'aiguille derrière la première maille et l'introduire dans la deuxième maille comme pour la tricoter à l'endroit. Tricoter à l'endroit cette deuxième maille sans la glisser de l'aiguille gauche ; puis tricoter à l'endroit la première maille en laissant glisser de l'aiguille en même temps la deuxième maille. Ceci forme un torse.

Chart Instructions in German
Strickschrift—Anweisungen in Deutsch

ALLGEMEINE ANWEISUNGEN ZUM LESEN DER STRICKSCHRIFT

Alle Zeilen der Strickschrift werden von rechts nach links gelesen. The leeren Kästchen in der Strickschrift haben keine Bedeutung.

Für Modelle, welche mit Hilfe von zwei Stricknadeln gearbeitet sind, jede Zeile der Strickschrift vertritt einen Mustersatz einer Musterreihe und ist mit einer Nummer versehen. Alle Zwischenreihen, die nicht nummeriert sind, werden links gestrickt.

Für Modelle, welche in der Runde gestrickt sind, jede nummerierte Zeile der Strickschrift ist ein Mustersatz einer Runde. Jede nicht bezeichnete Runde wird rechts gestrickt.

Die Teile der Strickschrift, welche mit einer Klammer oder einem Pfeil bezeichnet sind, werden in einer bestimmten Weise wiederholt. Die Anzahl dieser Wiederholungen des Mustersatzes ist in der schriftlichen Erklärung neben oder unter der Strickschrift gegeben und mit Hilfe der folgenden Ubersetzungen leicht zu folgen.

Die Maschenanzahl, welche nötig ist um die Modelle zu beginnen, kann von der schriftlichen Anweisung unter ' Casting-On " d.h. anschlagen, genommen werden.

Materials—Material.
Crochet Cotton—Häkelgarn.
Knitting Pins, Knitting Needles—Stricknadeln.
Circular Pin (Needle)—Strickring.
Crochet Hook—Häkelnadel
Measurements—Masse.
4 inches (ins.)—sind beiläufig 10 cm.
Casting-On—Anschlagen von Maschen.
Casting-Off—Abketten der Maschen.
Crocheting-Off—Abhäkeln.
Finishing—Fertigstellen.
Washing—Waschen.
Stretching—Spannen.
Knit (Knit plain) — Rechts stricken.
Purl—Links stricken.
Stitch (Stitches)—Strickmasche (Strickmaschen).
Chain—Luftmasche.
Double Crochet—Feste Masche (Häkelmasche).
Row—Musterreihe.
Round—Musterrunde.
Repeat—Wiederholen.
Once—Einmal.
Twice—Zweimal.
Times (3 times, 4 times etc.)—Mal (3 mal, 4 mal usw.)
Part—Teil.
Section—Abschnitt.

ZEICHENERKLARUNG

Eine Masche rechts stricken.

Eine Masche links stricken.

Eine Masche rechts verschränkt stricken, d.h. die Masche von ihrer Mitte nach hinten abstricken.

Einmal umschlagen. Sind mehrere Umschläge nebeneinander, so werden diese in der folgenden Reihe oder Runde abwechselnd rechts und links abgestrickt.

Eine Masche abheben.

Zwei Maschen rechts zusammenstricken.

Eine Masche abheben, die nächste Masche rechts stricken und dann die abgehobene Masche überziehen.

Eine Masche abheben, die zwei folgenden Maschen rechts zusammenstricken und dann die abgehobene Masche überziehen.

Zwei Maschen abheben, zwei Maschen rechts zusammenstricken und dann die zwei abgehobenen Maschen überziehen.

Aus einer Masche zwei Maschen stricken, und zwar eine Masche links und eine Masche rechts.

Aus einer Masche drei Maschen stricken, und zwar eine Masche rechts, eine Masche links und eine Masche rechts.

Aus dem Doppelumschlag der vorhergehenden Runde sechs Maschen stricken, und zwar abwechselnd eine Masche rechts und eine Masche links (Coronet Design). Aus dem Umschlag der vorhergehenden Runde 5 Maschen stricken (Sun Ray Design).

Zwei Maschen gekreuzt abstricken, d.h. zuerst den Faden wie zum Rechtsstricken durch die zweite und dann durch die erste Masche holen bevor man beide Maschen von der Nadel gleiten lässt.

X   Dieses Zeichen vor einer Musterrunde bedeutet, dass die erste Masche noch auf die vorhergehende Nadel gestrickt wird bevor man anfängt die gegebene Musterrunde zu arbeiten. Bei den anderen Nadeln verschiebt sich der Anfang genau so.

X X   Zwei solche Zeichen bedeuten, dass sich der Anfang der Runde um zwei Maschen verschiebt wie oben erklärt.

Diese kleinen Klammern über der letzten Zeile der Strickschrift geben die Anzahl der Strickmaschen, welche mit einer festen Masche zusammengehäkelt werden. Die Zahlen zwischen den Klammern geben die Anzahl der Luftmaschen, welche nötig sind für den Bogen von einer festen Masche zur anderen.

CHAPTER II

WORKING INSTRUCTIONS
FOR DESIGNS KNITTED ON TWO PINS

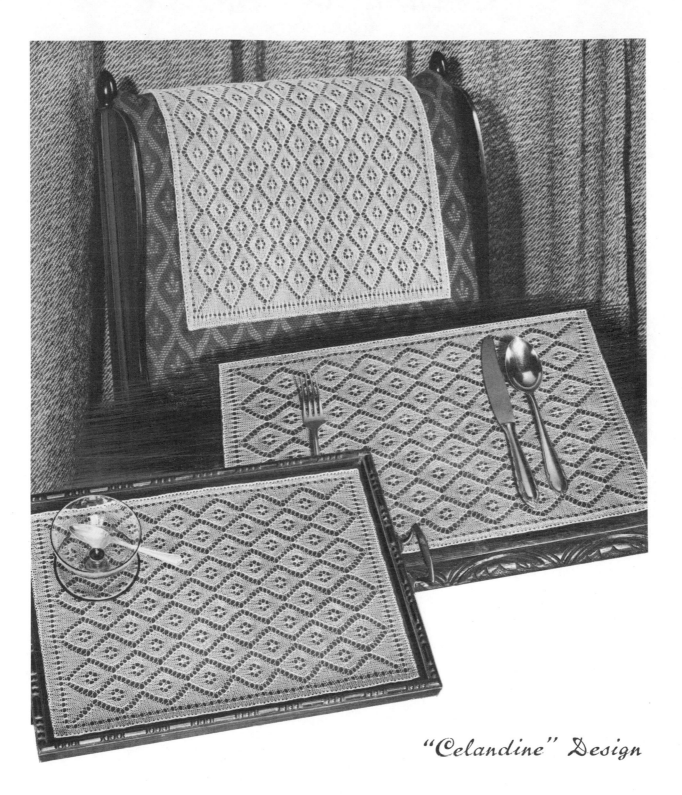

"Celandine" Design

"Celandine" Design

Tray Cloth—Luncheon Mat—Chair Back

MATERIALS:—

TRAY CLOTH—1 ball of Crochet Cotton No. 50.

LUNCHEON MAT—1 ball of Crochet Cotton No. 50.

CHAIR BACK—1 ball of Crochet Cotton No. 40.

Two knitting pins No. 13.

One steel crochet hook No. 4 or 5.

MEASUREMENTS:—

TRAY CLOTH—11 ins. by 15 ins.

LUNCHEON MAT—11 ins. by 17 ins.

CHAIR BACK—15 ins. by 15 ins.

The design can easily be adapted to other measurements as shown in paragraph ADAPTATION of PATTERN.

Tray Cloth

CASTING-ON:—

Commence by casting on 91 stitches, turn, and work one row plain, and then knit the first pattern row of PART A.

Notice—Every row of which the number is missing knit purl.

PART A.

1st row.—P.2, knit to the last two stitches, P.2.

3rd row.—As 1st row.

5th row.—P.2, K.2, (Yo., K.2 tog.) repeat to last three stitches, K.1, P.2.

7th row.—As first row.

9th row.—P.2, K.1, Sl.1, K.1, psso., Yo., K.1, Yo., Sl.1, K.1, psso., K.6, * K.5, K.2 tog., Yo., K.1, Yo., Sl. 1, K.1, psso., K.6, * rep. 3 times more from * to *, K.5, K.2 tog., Yo., K.1, Yo., K.2 tog., K.1, P.2.

11th row.—P.2, K.5, Yo., Sl. 1, K.1, psso., K.5, * K.4, K.2 tog., Yo., K.3, Yo., Sl.1, K.1, psso., K.5, * rep. 3 times more from * to *, K.4, K.2 tog., Yo., K.5, P.2.

13th row.—P.2, K.1, Sl.1, K.1, psso., Yo., K.3, Yo., Sl.1, K.1, psso., K.4, * K.3, K.2 tog., Yo., K.5, Yo., Sl.1, K.1, psso., K.4, * rep. 3 times more from * to *, K.3, K.2 tog., Yo., K.3, Yo., K.2 tog., K.1, P.2.

15th row.—P.2, K.7, Yo., Sl.1, K.1, psso., K.3, * K.2, K.2 tog., Yo., K.7, Yo., Sl.1, K.1, psso., K.3, * rep. 3 times more from * to *, K.2, K.2 tog., Yo., K.7, P.2.

17th row.—P.2, K.1, Sl.1, K.1, psso., Yo., K.5, Yo., Sl.1, K.1, psso., K.2, * K.1, K.2 tog., Yo., K.9, Yo., Sl.1, K.1, psso., K.2, * rep. 3 times more from * to *, K.1, K.2 tog., Yo., K.5, Yo., K.2 tog., K.1, P.2.

19th row.—P.2, K.9, Yo., Sl.1, K.1, psso., K.1, * K.2 tog., Yo., K.2 tog., K.3, Yo., K.1, Yo., K.3, Sl.1, K.1, psso., Yo., Sl.1, K.1, psso., K.1, * rep. 3 times more from * to *, K.2 tog., Yo., K.9, P.2.

21st row.—P.2, K.1, Sl.1, K.1, psso., Yo., K.7, Yo., Sl.1, K.2 tog., psso., * Yo., K.2 tog., K.3, (Yo., K.3) twice, Sl.1, K.1, psso., Yo., Sl.1, K.2 tog., psso., * rep. 3 times more from * to *, Yo., K.7, Yo., K.2 tog., K.1, P.2.

Now proceed with PART B.

PART B.

23rd row.—P.2, K.8, K.2 tog., Yo., K.2, * K.1, Yo., Sl.1, K.1, psso., K.3, Yo., Sl.1, K.2 tog., psso., Yo., K.3, K.2 tog., Yo., K.2, * rep. 3 times more from * to *, K.1, Yo., Sl.1, K.1, psso., K.8, P.2.

25th row.—P.2, K.1, Sl.1, K.1, psso., Yo., K.4, K.2 tog., Yo., K.3, * K.2, Yo., Sl.1, K.1, psso., K.7, K.2 tog., Yo., K.3, * rep. 3 times more from * to *, K.2, Yo., Sl.1, K.1, psso., K.4, Yo., K.2 tog., K.1, P.2.

27th row.—P.2, K.6, K.2 tog., Yo., K.4, * K.3, Yo., Sl.1, K.1, psso., K.5, K.2 tog., Yo., K.4, * rep. 3 times more from * to *, K.3, Yo., Sl.1, K.1, psso., K.6, P.2.

29th row.—P.2, K.1, Sl.1, K.1, psso., Yo., K.2, K.2 tog., Yo., K.5, * K.4, Yo., Sl.1, K.1, psso., K.3, K.2 tog., Yo., K.5, * rep. 3 times more from * to *, K.4, Yo., Sl.1, K.1, psso., K.2, Yo., K.2 tog., K.1, P.2.

31st row.—P.2, K.4, K.2 tog., Yo., K.2 tog., K.3, Yo., K.1, * Yo., K.3, Sl.1, K.1, psso., Yo., Sl.1, K.1, psso., K.1, K.2 tog., Yo., K.2 tog., K.3, Yo., K.1, * rep. 3 times more from * to *, Yo., K.3, Sl.1, K.1, psso., Yo., Sl.1, K.1, psso., K.4, P.2.

33rd row.—P.2, K.1, Sl.1, K.1, psso., (Yo., K.2 tog.,) twice, K.3, Yo., K.2, * K.1, Yo., K.3, Sl.1, K.1, psso., Yo., Sl.1, K.2 tog., psso., Yo., K.2 tog., K.3, Yo., K.2, * rep. 3 times more from * to *, K.1, Yo., K.3, (Sl.1, K.1, psso., Yo.) twice, K.2 tog., K.1, P.2.

35th row.—P.2, K.5, Yo., Sl.1, K.1, psso., K.3, Yo., Sl.1, K.2 tog., psso., * Yo., K.3, K.2 tog., Yo., K.3, Yo., Sl.1, K.1, psso., K.3, Yo., Sl.1, K.2 tog., psso., * rep. 3 times more from * to *, Yo., K.3, K.2 tog., Yo., K.5, P.2.

37th row.—as 13th row.

39th row.—as 15th row.

41st row.—as 17th row.

43rd row.—as 19th row.

45th row.—as 21st row.

After finishing purl row 46 work PART B rows 23 to 45 incl. 5 times more, and then proceed with PART C.

PART C.

47th row.—as 23rd row.

49th row.—as 25th row.

51st row.—as 27th row.

53rd row.—as 29th row.

55th row.—P.2, K.4, K.2 tog., Yo., K.6, * K.5, Yo., Sl.1, K.1, psso., K.1, K.2 tog., Yo., K.6, * rep. 3 times more from * to *, K.5, Yo., Sl.1, K.1, psso., K.4, P.2.

57th row.—P.2, K.1, Sl.1, K.1, psso., Yo., K.2 tog., Yo., K.7, * K.6, Yo., Sl. 1, K.2 tog., psso., Yo., K.7, * rep. 3 times more from * to *, K.6, Yo., Sl.1, K.1, psso., Yo., K.2 tog., K.1, P.2.

59th row.—P.2, knit plain to the last two stitches, P.2.

61st row.—P.2, K.2, (Yo., K.2 tog.,) repeat to the last three stitches, K.1, P.2.

63rd row.—As 59th row.

65th row.—As 59th row.

66th row.—Knit plain.

FINISHING OF TRAY CLOTH.

After working row 66, turn, and with the right side of the work facing, cast off the stitches very loosely. At the end of the row do not break off the thread, but work all round the cloth a row of double crochet to give the lace a firmer finish.

Along the side edges crochet 2 d.c. into the space between each little rib formed by the garter stitch, used along the right and left hand border. Along the cast-on and cast-off edge work just 1 d.c. into each stitch, taking care that the edge is not pulled tight but stretches to the proper measurements. The corners should be turned with 3 double crochet. Having thus worked all round the cloth finish with a slip stitch into the first d.c., break off and secure thread invisibly.

STRETCHING OF TRAY CLOTH.

Prepare paper pattern by drawing an oblong 11 ins. by 15 ins. Take the lace cloth which has been washed and starched and pin down the corners first. Then pin out the cloth along the edges in regular spaces of about 1 in., using the strong edge of the double crochet to insert the pins. Finish by treating the lace according to BASIC

INSTRUCTIONS. Since the border of the TRAY CLOTH is not scalloped but all straight, it is quite suitable to iron the washed and starched lace into shape.

Luncheon Mat

Work exactly to directions given for the knitting of TRAY CLOTH but with one alteration ; PART B has to be worked 7 times altogether and not 6 times, as stated in the pattern. This extra repetition adds 2 ins. to the lace cloth.

Finish as for the TRAY CLOTH.

The paper pattern drawn out for the stretching of the MAT has to be an oblong 11 ins. by 17 ins.

Chair Back

Commence by casting on 123 stitches. Then work PARTS A, B, and C according to the instructions for TRAY CLOTH, but notice that the section between the asterisks has to be worked 6 times in each pattern line instead of 4 times. This refers to each PART of the pattern. Finish as for TRAY CLOTH.

The paper pattern prepared for the pinning out is a square of 15 ins.

Adaptation of Pattern

The pattern " CELANDINE " is made up of the Border and a Middle Panel, the latter being composed of the section within the asterisks. With altering the number of middle sections the width of the lace cloth alters accordingly.

The borders on the right and left measure together 3 ins., and 27 sts. are needed for the start. One middle section requires 16 sts. and measures 2 ins. It is therefore possible to cast on as many times 16 sts. as the width of the lace cloth to be worked requires, remembering, that an extra 3 ins. will be added by the border on each side.

The length of the pattern is governed by the repetition of PART B, one repeat measuring 2 ins. PARTS A and C, which form the border on top and bottom measure together 3 ins.

Finish as for TRAY CLOTH.

In this manner various articles can be worked using the instructions for the TRAY CLOTH, and the pattern is quite suitable for working a Runner or even a smaller Table Cloth.

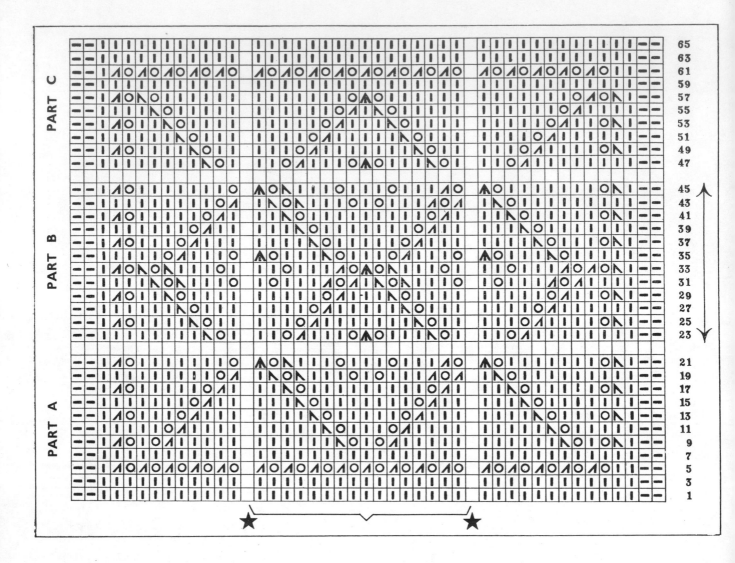

Chart for Design "Celandine"

Every row of which the number is missing work purl, but the finishing row 66 knit plain.

TRAY CLOTH:—

Work PART A, PART B 6 times, PART C.

Every chart line to be knitted once in one row, but work the section from * to * 4 times.

LUNCHEON MAT:—

Same as for TRAY CLOTH but work PART B 7 times.

CHAIR BACK:—

Work PART A, PART B 6 times, PART C, but knit the section from * to * 6 times in each pattern row.

"Mosaic" Design

Trolley Cloth—Tea Cosy—Table Cloth

MATERIALS:—

TROLLEY CLOTH—1 ball of Crochet Cotton No. 50.

TABLE CLOTH—5 balls of Crochet Cotton No. 50.

2 knitting pins No. 13, one steel crochet hook No. 5.

TEA COSY—1 ball of Crochet Cotton No. 50.
4 double pointed knitting needles No. 13, length 12 ins.
One steel crochet hook No. 5.

MEASUREMENTS:—

TROLLEY CLOTH—13 ins. by 21 ins.
TEA COSY—About 8½ ins. high, 12 ins. wide.
TABLE CLOTH—40 ins. square.

The sizes of TROLLEY CLOTH and TEA COSY, as well as of the TABLE CLOTH, can easily be altered to other measurements as explained in paragraph ADAPT-ATION of PATTERN.

Trolley Cloth

CASTING-ON:—

Commence by casting on 107 stitches, turn, and work one row plain.

Now knit first pattern row of following PART A.

Every row of which the number is missing work purl.

PART A.

1st row.—P.2, knit to the last two stitches, P.2.

3rd row.—As first row.

5th row.—P.2, K.2, (Yo., K.2 tog.) repeat to last three stitches, K.1, P.2.

7th row.—as first row.

9th row.—P.2, K.1, Sl.1, K.1, psso., Yo., K.1, Yo., Sl.1, K.1, psso., K.6, * K.5, K.2 tog., Yo., K.1, Yo., Sl.1, K.1, psso., K.6, * rep. 4 times more from * to *, K.5, K.2 tog., Yo., K.1, Yo., K.2 tog., K.1, P.2.

11th row.—P.2, K.5, Yo., Sl.1, K.1, psso., K.5, * K.4, K.2 tog., Yo., K.3, Yo., Sl.1, K.1, psso., K.5, * rep. 4 times more from * to *, K.4, K.2 tog., Yo., K.5, P.2.

13th row.—P.2, K.1, Sl.1, K.1, psso., Yo., K.3, Yo., Sl.1, K.1, psso., K.4, * K.3, K.2 tog., Yo., K.5, Yo., Sl.1, K.1, psso., K.4, * rep. 4 times more from * to *, K.3, K.2 tog., Yo., K.3, Yo., K.2 tog., K.1, P.2.

15th row.—P.2, K.7, Yo., Sl.1, K.1, psso., K.3, * K.2, K.2 tog., Yo., K.7, Yo., Sl.1, K.1, psso., K.3, * rep. 4 times more from * to *, K.2, K.2 tog., Yo., K.7, P.2.

17th row.—P.2, K.1, Sl.1, K.1, psso., Yo., K.5, Yo., Sl.1, K.1, psso., K.2, * K.1, K.2 tog., Yo., K.9, Yo., Sl.1, K.1, psso., K.2, * rep. 4 times more from * to *, K.1, K.2 tog., Yo., K.5, Yo., K.2 tog., K.1, P.2.

19th row.—P.2, K.9, Yo., Sl.1, K.1, psso., K.1, * K.2 tog., Yo., K.1, Yo., Sl.1, K.1, psso., K.5, K.2 tog., Yo., K.1, Yo., Sl.1, K.1, psso., K.1, * rep. 4 times more from * to *, K.2 tog., Yo., K.9, P.2.

21st row.—P.2, K.1, Sl.1, K.1, psso., Yo., K.7, Yo., Sl.1, K.2 tog., psso., * Yo., K.1, (Yo., Sl.1, K.1, psso.) twice, K.3, (K.2 tog., Yo.) twice, K.1, Yo., Sl.1, K.2 tog., psso., * rep. 4 times more from * to *, Yo., K.7, Yo., K.2 tog., K.1, P.2.

Proceed with PART B.

PART B.

23rd row.—P.2, K.8, K.2 tog., Yo., K.2, * K.1, (Yo., Sl.1, K.1, psso.) 3 times, K.1, (K.2 tog., Yo.) 3 times, K.2, * rep. 4 times more from * to *, K.1, Yo., Sl.1, K.1, psso., K.8, P.2.

25th row.—P.2, K.1, Sl.1, K.1, psso., Yo., K.4, K.2 tog., Yo., K.3, * K.2, (Yo., Sl.1, K.1, psso.) twice, Yo., Sl.1, K.2 tog., psso., (Yo., K.2 tog.) twice, Yo., K.3, * rep. 4 times more from * to *, K.2, Yo., Sl.1, K.1, psso., K.4, Yo., K.2 tog., K.1, P.2.

27th row.—P.2, K.6, K.2 tog., Yo., K.4, * K.3, (Yo., Sl.1, K.1, psso.) twice, K.1, (K.2 tog., Yo.) twice, K.4, * rep. 4 times more from * to *, K.3, Yo., Sl.1, K.1, psso., K.6, P.2.

29th row.—P.2, K.1, Sl.1, K.1, psso., Yo., K.2, K.2 tog., Yo., K.5, * K.4, Yo., Sl.1, K.1, psso., Yo., Sl.1, K.2 tog., psso., Yo., K.2 tog., Yo., K.5, * rep. 4 times more from

* to *, K.4, Yo., Sl.1, K.1, psso., K.2, Yo., K.2 tog., K.1, P.2.

31st row.—P.2, K.4, K.2 tog., Yo., K.1, Yo., Sl.1, K.1, psso., K.3, * K.2, (K.2 tog., Yo., K.1, Yo., Sl.1, K.1, psso., K.1) twice, K.2, * rep. 4 times more from * to *, K.2, K.2 tog., Yo., K.1, Yo., Sl.1, K.1, psso., K.4, P.2.

33rd row.—P.2, K.1, Sl.1, K.1, psso., Yo., K.2, tog. Yo., K.1, (Yo., Sl.1, K.1, psso.) twice, K.2, * K.1, (K.2 tog., Yo.) twice, K.1, Yo., Sl.1, K.2 tog., psso., Yo., K.1, (Yo., Sl.1, K.1, psso.) twice, K.2, * rep. 4 times more from * to *, K.1, (K.2 tog., Yo.) twice, K.1, Yo., Sl.1, K.1, psso., Yo., K.2 tog., K.1, P.2.

35th row.—P.2, K.5, (Yo., Sl.1, K.1, psso.) 3 times, K.1, * (K.2 tog., Yo.) 3 times, K.3, (Yo., Sl.1, K.1, psso.) 3 times, K.1, * rep. 4 times more from * to *, (K.2 tog., Yo.) 3 times, K.5, P.2.

37th row.—P.2, K.1, Sl.1, K.1, psso., Yo., K.3, (Yo., Sl.1, K.1, psso.) twice, Yo., Sl.1, K.2 tog., psso., * (Yo., K.2 tog.) twice, Yo., K.5, (Yo., Sl.1, K.1, psso.) twice, Yo., Sl.1, K.2 tog., psso., * rep. 4 times more from * to *, (Yo., K.2 tog.) twice, Yo., K.3, Yo., K.2 tog., K.1, P.2.

39th row.—P.2, K.7, (Yo., Sl.1, K.1, psso.) twice, K.1, * (K.2 tog., Yo.) twice, K.7, (Yo., Sl.1, K.1, psso.) twice, K.1, * rep. 4 times more from * to *, (K.2 tog., Yo.) twice, K.7, P.2.

41st row.—P.2, K.1, Sl.1, K.1, psso., Yo., K.5, Yo., Sl.1, K.1, psso., Yo., Sl.1, K.2 tog., psso., * Yo., K.2 tog., Yo., K.9, Yo., Sl.1, K.1, psso., Yo., Sl.1, K.2 tog., psso., * rep. 4 times more from * to *, Yo., K.2, tog., Yo., K.5, Yo., K.2 tog., K.1, P.2.

43rd row.—P.2, K.9, Yo., Sl.1, K.1, psso., K.1, * K.2 tog., Yo., K.1, Yo., Sl.1, K.1, psso., K.5, K.2 tog., Yo., K.1, Yo., Sl.1, K.1, psso., K.1, * rep. 4 times more from * to *, K.2 tog., Yo., K.9, P.2.

45th row.—P.2, K.1, Sl.1, K.1, psso., Yo., K.7, Yo., Sl.1, K.2 tog., psso., * Yo., K.1, (Yo., Sl.1, K.1, psso.) twice, K.3, (K.2 tog., Yo.) twice, K.1, Yo., Sl.1, K.2 tog., psso., * rep. 4 times more from * to *, Yo., K.7, Yo., K.2 tog., K.1, P.2.

After knitting purl row 46 work PART B rows 23 to 45 incl. 8 times more which brings the rows up to 237. Then proceed with PART C.

PART C.

239th row.—as 23rd row.

241st row.—as 25th row.

243rd row.—as 27th row.

245th row.—as 29th row.

247th row.—P.2, K.4, K.2 tog., Yo., K.6, * K.5, Yo., Sl.1. K.1, psso., K.1, K.2 tog., Yo., K.6, * rep. 4 times more from * to *, K.5, Yo., Sl.1, K.1, psso., K.4, P.2.

249th row.—P.2, K.1, Sl.1, K.1, psso., Yo., K.2 tog., Yo., K.7, * K.6, Yo., Sl.1, K.2 tog., psso., Yo., K.7, * rep. 4 times more from * to *, K.6, Yo., Sl.1, K.1, psso., Yo., K.2 tog., K.1, P.2.

251st row.—P.2, knit plain to the last two stitches, P.2.

253rd row.—P.2, K.2, (Yo., K.2 tog.) repeat to the last 3 stitches, K.1, P.2.

255th row.—as 251st row.

257th row.—as 251st row.

258th row.—Knit plain.

FINISHING OF TROLLEY CLOTH.

After working row 258, turn, and with the right side of the work facing, cast off the stitches very loosely. At the end of the row do not break off the thread, but work all round the cloth a row of double crochet to give the lace a firmer finish.

Along the side edges crochet 2 d.c. into the space between each little rib formed by the garter stitch, used along the right and left hand border. Along the cast-on and cast-off edge work just 1 d.c. into each stitch, taking care that the edge is not pulled tight but stretches to the proper measurements. The corners should be turned with 3 double crochet. Having thus worked all round the cloth finish with a slip stitch into the first d.c., break off, and secure thread invisibly.

STRETCHING OF TROLLEY CLOTH.

Prepare paper pattern by drawing an oblong 21 ins. by 13 ins. Take the lace cloth which has been washed and starched and pin down the corners first. Then pin out the cloth along the edges in regular spaces of about 1 in., using the strong edge of the double crochet to insert the pins.

Finish by treating the lace according to BASIC INSTRUCTIONS.

Since the border of the cloth is not scalloped but all straight, it is quite suitable to iron the washed and starched lace into shape.

Adaptation of Pattern

The adaptation of this pattern is exactly the same as for the pattern "CELANDINE," since the same number of stitches were used to compose the two designs.

See therefore ADAPTATION OF PATTERN "CELANDINE."

Notice further that the instructions for Casting-On of the Celandine Tray Cloth, Luncheon Mat and Chair Back could be used to make the same articles to the same measurements in the MOSAIC pattern.

The repetition of PART B and the repeat of the section between the asterisks will be the same as given in the Celandine patterns.

Table Cloth

Commence by casting on 315 stitches. Then work PART A, PART B 18 times and PART C according to the instructions for TROLLEY CLOTH, but notice that the section between the asterisks has to be worked 18 times in each pattern line instead of 6 times. This refers to each PART of the pattern. Finish as for TROLLEY CLOTH.

The paper pattern prepared for the pinning out is a square of 40 ins.

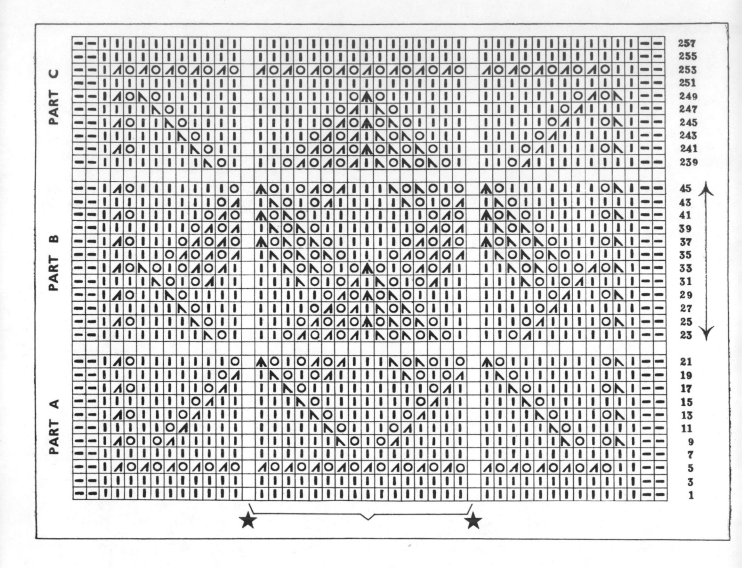

Chart for "Mosaic" Trolley Cloth and Table Cloth

TROLLEY CLOTH:

Work PART A, PART B 9 times, PART C.

Every chart line to be knitted once in one row, but work the section from * to * 5 times.

Every row of which the number is missing work purl, but knit last row 258.

TABLE CLOTH:

Work PART A, PART B 18 times, PART C.

Every chart line to be knitted once in one row, but work the section from * to * 18 times.

Every row of which the number is missing work purl, but knit last row.

Tea Cosy

Commence at the base of the COSY by casting on 192 stitches on to three needles having 64 stitches on each needle. Arrange the needles to a circle (like working a sock), and knit six rounds in RIB K.2, P.2. Then work (Yo., K.2 tog.) to the end of round followed by another six rounds plain. Now knit 1st pattern round of PART A.

Notice.—Every round of which the number is missing, knit plain.

PART A.

Knit each section from [to] 12 times in one round.

1st round.—(Yo., K.2 tog.) to the end of round.
3 rounds plain.

5th round.—[Sl.1, K.1, psso., K.11, K.2 tog., Yo., K.1, Yo.].

7th round.—[Sl.1, K.1, psso., K.9, K.2 tog., Yo., K.3, Yo.]

9th round.—[Sl.1, K.1, psso., K.7, K.2 tog., Yo., K.5, Yo.]

11th round.—[Sl.1, K.1, psso., K.5, K.2 tog., Yo., K.7, Yo.]

13th round.—[Sl.1, K.1, psso., K.3, K.2 tog., Yo., K.9, Yo.]

15th round.—[Sl.1, K.1, psso., K.1, K.2 tog., Yo., K.1, Yo., Sl.1, K.1, psso., K.5, K.2 tog., Yo., K.1, Yo.]

17th round.—[Yo., Sl.1, K.2, tog., psso., Yo., K.1, (Yo., Sl.1, K.1, psso.) twice, K.3, (K.2 tog., Yo.) twice, K.1].
Proceed with PART B.

PART B.

Knit each section from [to] 12 times in one round.

19th round.—[Yo., K.3, (Yo., Sl.1, K.1, psso.) 3 times, K.1, (K.2 tog., Yo.) twice, K.2 tog.]

21st round.—[Yo., K.5, (Yo., Sl.1, K.1, psso.) twice, Yo., Sl.1, K.2 tog., psso., (Yo., K.2 tog.) twice.]

23rd round.—[Yo., K.7, (Yo., Sl.1, K.1, psso.) twice, K.1, K.2 tog., Yo., K.2 tog.]

25th round.—[Yo., K.9, Yo., Sl.1, K.1, psso., Yo., Sl.1, K.2 tog., psso., Yo. K.2 tog.]

27th round.—[Yo., K.1, Yo., Sl.1, K.1, psso., K.5, K.2 tog., Yo., K.1, Yo., Sl.1, K.1, psso., K.1, K.2 tog.]

29th round.—[K.1, (Yo., Sl.1, K.1, psso.) twice, K.3, (K.2 tog., Yo.) twice, K.1, Yo., Sl.1, K.2 tog., psso., Yo.]

31st round.—[(Sl.1, K.1, psso., Yo.) twice, Sl.1, K.1, psso., K.1, (K.2 tog., Yo.) 3 times, K.3, Yo.]

33rd round.—[(Sl.1, K.1, psso., Yo.) twice, Sl.1, K.2 tog., psso., (Yo., K.2 tog.) twice, Yo., K.5, Yo.]

35th round.—[Sl.1, K.1, psso., Yo., Sl.1, K.1, psso., K.1, (K.2 tog., Yo.) twice, K.7, Yo.]

37th round.—[Sl.1, K.1, psso., Yo., Sl.1, K.2 tog., psso., Yo., K.2 tog., Yo., K.9, Yo.]

39th round.—[Sl.1, K.1, psso., K.1, K.2 tog., Yo., K.1, Yo., Sl.1, K.1, psso., K.5, K.2 tog., Yo., K.1, Yo.]

41st round.—[Yo., Sl.1, K.2 tog., psso., Yo., K.1, (Yo., Sl.1, K.1, psso.) twice, K.3, (K.2 tog., Yo.) twice, K.1.]

Now knit once more PART B rounds 19 to 41 incl. and then follow instructions of PART C.

PART C.

Knit each section from [to] twice in one round.

67th round.—[Yo., Sl.1, K.2, tog. psso., (Yo., Sl.1, K.1, psso.) 3 times, K.1, (K.2 tog., Yo.) 3 times, K.2, * K.1, (Yo., Sl.1, K.1, psso.) 3 times, K.1, (K.2 tog., Yo.) 3 times, K.2, * rep. 3 times more from * to *, K.1, (Yo., Sl.1, K.1, psso.) 3 times, K.1, (K.2 tog., Yo.) twice, K.2 tog.]

69th round.—[Yo., Sl.1, K.2 tog., psso., (Yo., Sl.1, K.1, psso.) twice, Yo., Sl.1, K.2 tog., psso., (Yo., K.2 tog.) twice, Yo., K.3, * K.2, (Yo., Sl.1, K.1, psso.) twice, Yo., Sl.1, K.2 tog., psso., (Yo., K.2 tog.) twice, Yo., K.3, * rep. 3 times more from * to *, K.2, (Yo., Sl.1, K.1, psso.) twice, Yo., Sl.1, K.2 tog., psso., (Yo., K.2 tog.) twice.]

71st round.—[Yo., Sl.1, K.2 tog., psso., (Yo., Sl.1, K.1, psso.) twice, K.1, (K.2 tog., Yo.) twice, K.4, * K.3, (Yo., Sl.1, K.1, psso.) twice, K.1, (K.2 tog., Yo.) twice, K.4, * rep. 3 times more from * to *, K.3, (Yo., Sl.1, K.1, psso.) twice, K.1, K.2 tog., Yo., K.2 tog.]

73rd round.—[Yo., Sl.1, K.2, tog. psso., Yo., Sl.1, K.1, psso., Yo., Sl.1, K.2 tog., psso., Yo., K.2 tog., Yo., K.5, * K.4, Yo., Sl.1, K.1, psso., Yo., Sl.1, K.2 tog., psso., Yo., K.2 tog., Yo., K.5, * rep. 3 times more from * to *, K.4, Yo., Sl.1, K.1, psso., Yo., Sl.1, K.2 tog., psso., Yo., K.2 tog.]

75th round.—[Yo., Sl.1, K.2 tog., psso., Yo., Sl.1, K.1, psso., K.1, K.2 tog., Yo., K.1, Yo., Sl.1, K.1, psso., K.3, * K.2, (K.2 tog., Yo., K.1, Yo., Sl.1, K.1, psso., K.1) twice, K.2, * rep. 3 times more from * to *, K.2, K.2 tog., Yo., K.1, Yo., Sl.1, K.1, psso., K.1, K.2 tog.]

77th round.—[(Yo., Sl.1, K.2 tog., psso.) twice, Yo., K.1, (Yo., Sl.1, K.1, psso.) twice, K.2, * K.1, (K.2 tog., Yo.) twice, K.1, Yo., Sl.1, K.2 tog., psso., Yo., K.1, (Yo., Sl.1, K.1, psso.) twice, K.2, * rep. 3 times more from * to *, K.1, (K.2 tog., Yo.) twice, K.1, Yo., Sl.1, K.2 tog., psso.]

79th round.—[Yo., Sl.1, K.2 tog., psso., (Yo., Sl.1, K.1, psso.) 4 times, K.1, * (K.2 tog., Yo.) 3 times, K.3, (Yo., Sl.1, K.1, psso.) 3 times, K.1, * rep. 3 times more from * to *, (K.2 tog., Yo.) 3 times, K.2 tog.]

81st round.—[Yo., Sl.1, K.2 tog., psso., (Yo., Sl.1, K.1, psso.) 3 times, Yo., Sl.1, K.2 tog., psso., * (Yo., K.2 tog.) twice, Yo., K.5, (Yo., Sl.1, K.1, psso.) twice, Yo., Sl.1, K.2 tog., psso., * rep. 3 times more from * to *, (Yo., K.2 tog.) 3 times.]

83rd round.—[Yo., Sl.1, K.2 tog., psso., (Yo., Sl.1, K.1, psso.) 3 times, K.1, * (K.2 tog., Yo.)twice, K.7, (Yo., Sl.1, K.1, psso.) twice, K.1, * rep. 3 times more from * to *, (K.2 tog., Yo.) twice, K.2 tog.]

85th round.—[Yo., Sl.1, K.2 tog., psso., (Yo., Sl.1, K.1, psso.) twice, Yo., Sl.1, K.2 tog., psso., * Yo., K.2 tog., Yo., K.9, Yo., Sl.1, K.1, psso., Yo., Sl.1, K.2 tog., psso., * rep. 3 times more from * to *, (Yo., K.2 tog.) twice.]

87th round.—[Yo., Sl.1, K.2 tog., psso., (Yo., Sl.1., K.1, psso.) twice, K.1, * K.2 tog., Yo., K.11, Yo., Sl.1, K.1, psso., K.1, * rep. 3 times more from * to *, K.2 tog., Yo., K.2 tog.]

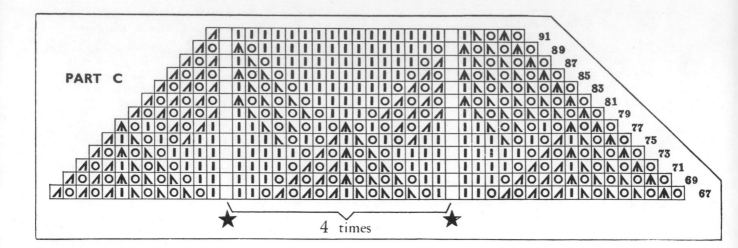

PART C

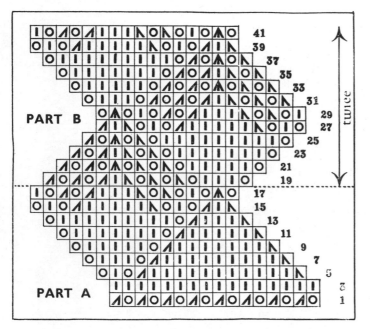

Every round of which the number is missing knit plain. Work PART A, PART B twice. and then PART C.

PART A AND PART B :—
Every chart line to be knitted 12 times in one round.

PART C:—
Every chart line to be knitted twice in one round, but knit the section within the bracket as many times as indicated by the number below.

Adaptation of Pattern for Tea Cosy

The TEA COSY can easily be worked to a larger size by casting on another 32 sts. in addition to the given number, which will add another 2 ins. to the width.

Then work exactly according to the instructions, but notice that the pattern lines of PARTS A and B will repeat 14 times instead of 12 times in one round.

In PART C the repeat of the section from * to * will increase by one.

The COSY can be made higher by repeating PART B rounds 19 to 41 incl. as often as wished. Each such repetition adds another 2 ins. to the height.

STRETCHING OF COSY.

Use thick starch for the final rinse after washing, squeeze gently and pull the lace cover nicely into shape, placing it on a clean cloth or towel. When almost dry press carefully, stretching the lace at the same time.

The finished lace cover can then be pulled over a cosy of coloured felt of the same shape and measurements.

89th round.—[Yo., Sl.1, K.2 tog., psso., Yo., Sl.1, K.1, psso., Yo., Sl.1, K.2 tog., psso., * Yo., K.13, Yo., Sl.1, K.2 tog., psso., * rep. 3 times more from * to *, Yo., K.2 tog.]

91st round.—[Yo., Sl.1, K.2 tog., psso., Yo., Sl.1, K.1, psso., K.65, K.2 tog.]

92nd round.—Knit plain.

FINISHING OF COSY.

After last plain round 92 the COSY can be finished in different ways. The stitches left on the needles can be grafted together as is usually done with the toe of a sock. Another method could be used by casting off (rather loosely) all stitches left on the needles and then crochet or stitch together the corresponding stitches from each side.

It is also advisable to work one row of Double Crochet into each casting-on stitch at the base of the COSY to provide a firmer edge.

Secure threads invisibly.

"Rose Leaf" Design
Chair Set

"Rose Leaf" Design

Chair Set and Settee Back

MATERIALS:—

CHAIR BACK and two ARM RESTS—3 balls of Crochet Cotton No. 40.

SETTEE BACK—2 balls of Crochet Cotton No. 40. 2 knitting pins No. 12, one steel crochet hook No. 4.

MEASUREMENTS:—

CHAIR BACK—16 ins. by 16 ins.

ARM REST—12 ins. by 12 ins.

SETTEE BACK—32 ins. by 16 ins.

The pattern can easily be adapted to other measurements. See ADAPTATION of PATTERN.

Chair Back

CASTING-ON:—

Commence by casting on 122 stitches, turn, work one row plain and then knit the first pattern row of following PART A.

Every row of which the number is missing work purl.

PART A.

1st row.—P.3, (Yo., K.2 tog.) to last 3 stitches, P.3.

3rd row.—P.3, knit to last 3 stitches, P.3.

5th row and 7th row.—as 3rd row.

9th row.—as 1st row.

11th row, 13th row and 15th row.—as 3rd row.

17th row.—P.3, Sl.1, K.1, psso., * Yo., Sl.1, K.1, psso., K.5, (Yo., Sl.1, K.1, psso., K.3, K.2 tog.) twice, Yo., K.5, K.2 tog., * rep. 3 times more from * to *, Yo., K.2 tog., P.3.

19th row.—P.3, K.1, Yo., * K.1B, Yo., Sl.1, K.1, psso., K.5, (Yo., Sl.1, K.1, psso., K.1, K.2 tog., Yo., K.1) twice, K.4, K.2 tog., Yo., * rep. 3 times more from * to *, K.1B, Yo., K.1, P.3.

21st row.—P.3, Sl.1, K.1, psso., Yo., * K.2, Yo., Sl.1, K.1, psso., K.5, Yo., Sl.1, K.2 tog., psso., Yo., K.3, Yo., Sl.1, K.2 tog., psso., Yo., K.5, K. 2 tog., Yo., K.1, * rep. 3 times more from * to *, K.1, Yo., K.2 tog., P.3.

23rd row.—P.3, Sl.1, K.1, psso., Yo., * K.1B, Yo., K.2, Yo., Sl.1, K.1, psso., K.5, Yo., Sl.1, K.1, psso., K.3, K.2 tog., Yo., K.5, K.2 tog., Yo., K.2, Yo., * rep. 3 times more from * to *, K.1B, Yo., K.2 tog., P.3.

25th row.—P.3, Sl.1, K.1, psso., Yo., * K.1B., Yo., K.2 tog., K.2, Yo., Sl.1, K.1, psso., K.5, Yo., Sl.1, K.1, psso., K.1, K.2 tog., Yo., K.5, K.2 tog., Yo., K.2, Sl.1, K.1, psso., Yo., * rep. 3 times more from * to *, K.1B., Yo., K.2 tog., P.3.

27th row.—P.3, Sl.1, K.1, psso., Yo., * K.1B., Yo., K.2 tog., K.1, Sl.1, K.1, psso., Yo., Sl.1, K.1, psso., K.5, Yo., Sl.1, K.2 tog., psso., Yo., K.5, K.2 tog., Yo., K.2 tog., K.1, Sl.1, K.1, psso., Yo., * rep. 3 times more from * to *, K.1B., Yo., K.2 tog., P.3.

29th row.—P.3, Sl.1, K.1, psso., Yo., * K.1B., Yo., K.2 tog., Yo., K.1B., Yo., Sl.1, K.1, psso., Yo., Sl.1, K.1, psso., K.11, K.2 tog., Yo., K.2 tog., Yo., K.1B., Yo., Sl.1, K.1, psso., Yo., * rep. 3 times more from * to *, K.1B., Yo., K.2 tog., P.3.

31st row.—P.3, Sl.1, K.1, psso., Yo., * K.1B., Yo., K.2 tog., K.1, Yo., K.1B., Yo., K.1, Sl.1, K.1, psso., Yo., Sl.1, K.1, psso., K.9, K.2 tog., Yo., K.2 tog., K.1, Yo., K.1B., Yo., K.1, Sl.1, K.1, psso., Yo., * rep. 3 times more from * to *, K.1B., Yo., K.2 tog., P.3.

33rd row.—P.3, Sl.1, K.1, psso., Yo., * K.1B., Yo., K.2 tog., K.2, Yo., K.1B., Yo., K.2, Sl.1, K.1, psso., Yo., Sl.1, K.1, psso., K.7, K.2 tog., Yo., K.2 tog., K.2, Yo., K.1B., Yo., K.2, Sl.1, K.1, psso., Yo., * rep. 3 times more from * to *, K.1B., Yo., K.2 tog., P.3.

35th row.—P.3, Sl.1, K.1, psso., Yo., * K.1B., Yo., K.2 tog., K.3, Yo., K.1B., Yo., K.3, Sl.1, K.1, psso., Yo., Sl.1, K.1, psso., K.5, K.2 tog., Yo., K.2 tog., K.3, Yo., K.1B., Yo., K.3, Sl.1, K.1, psso., Yo., * rep. 3 times more from * to *, K.1B., Yo., K.2 tog., P.3.

37th row.—P.3, Sl.1, K.1, psso., Yo., * K.1B., Yo., K.2 tog., K.9, Sl.1, K.1, psso., Yo., Sl.1, K.1, psso., K.3, K.2 tog., Yo., K.2 tog., K.9, Sl.1, K.1, psso., Yo., * rep. 3 times more from * to *, K.1B., Yo., K.2 tog., P.3.

39th row.—P.3, Sl.1, K.1, psso., Yo., * K.1B., Yo., K.2 tog., K.9, Sl.1, K.1, psso., Yo., Sl.1, K.1, psso., K.1, K.2 tog., Yo., K.2 tog., K.9, Sl.1, K.1, psso., Yo., * rep. 3 times more from * to *, K.1B., Yo., K.2 tog., P.3.

41st row.—P.3, Sl.1, K.1, psso., Yo., * K.1B., Yo., K.2 tog., K.9, Sl.1, K.1, psso., Yo., Sl.1, K.2 tog., psso., Yo., K.2 tog., K.9, Sl.1, K.1, psso., Yo., * rep. 3 times more from * to *, K.1B., Yo., K.2 tog., P.3.

Proceed with PART B.

PART B.

43rd row.—P.3, Sl.1, K.1, psso., Yo., * K.2, Yo., Sl.1, K.1, psso., K.7, K.2 tog., Yo., Sl.1, K.2, tog. psso., Yo., Sl.1, K.1, psso., K.7, K.2 tog., Yo., K.1, * rep. 3 times more from * to *, K.1, Yo., K.2 tog., P.3.

45th row.—P.3, Sl.1, K.1, psso., Yo., * K.1B., Yo., K.2, Yo., Sl.1, K.1, psso., K.5, K.2 tog., Yo., K.3, Yo., Sl.1, K.1, psso., K.5, K.2 tog., Yo., K.2, Yo., * rep. 3 times more from * to *, K.1B., Yo., K.2 tog., P.3.

47th row.—P.3, Sl.1, K.1, psso., Yo., * K.1B., Yo., K.2 tog., K.2, Yo., Sl.1, K.1, psso., K.3, K.2 tog., Yo., K.5, Yo., Sl.1, K.1, psso., K.3, K.2 tog., Yo., K.2, Sl.1, K.1, psso., Yo., * rep. 3 times more from * to *, K.1B., Yo., K.2 tog., P.3.

49th row.—P.3, Sl.1, K.1, psso., Yo., * K.1B., Yo., K.2 tog., K.1, Sl.1, K.1, psso., Yo., (Sl.1, K.1, psso., K.1, K.2 tog., Yo., K.1, Yo.) twice, Sl.1, K.1, psso., K.1, K.2 tog., Yo., K.2 tog., K.1, Sl.1, K.1, psso., Yo., * rep. 3 times more from * to *, K.1B., Yo., K.2 tog., P.3.

51st row.—P.3, Sl.1, K.1, psso., Yo., * K.1B., Yo., K.2 tog., Yo., K.1B., Yo., Sl.1, K.1, psso., Yo., (Sl.1, K.2 tog., psso., Yo., K.3, Yo.) twice, Sl.1, K.2 tog., psso., Yo., K.2 tog., Yo., K.1B., Yo., Sl.1, K.1, psso., Yo., * rep. 3 times more from * to *, K.1B., Yo., K.2 tog., P.3.

53rd row.—P.3, Sl.1, K.1, psso., Yo., * K.1B., Yo., K.2 tog., K.1, Yo., K.1B., Yo., K.1, Sl.1, K.1, psso., Yo., Sl.1, K.1, psso. K.4, Yo., K.1B., Yo., K.4, K.2 tog., Yo., K.2 tog., K.1, Yo., K.1B., Yo., K.1, Sl.1, K.1, psso., Yo., * rep. 3 times more from * to *, K.1B., Yo., K.2 tog., P.3.

55th row.—P.3, Sl.1, K.1, psso., Yo., * K.1B., Yo., K.2 tog., K.2, Yo., K.1B., Yo., K.2, Sl.1, K.1, psso., Yo., Sl.1, K.1, psso., K.1, K.2 tog., Yo., Sl.1, K.2 tog., psso., Yo., Sl.1, K.1, psso., K.1, K.2 tog., Yo., K.2, K.1B., Yo., K.2, Sl.1, K.1, psso., Yo., * rep. 3 times more from * to *, K.1B., Yo., K.2 tog., P.3.

57th row.—P.3, Sl.1, K.1, psso., Yo., * K.1B., Yo., K.2 tog., K.3, Yo., K.1B., Yo., K.3, Sl.1, K.1, psso., Yo., Sl.1, K.2 tog., psso., Yo., K.3, Yo., Sl.1, .K.2 tog., psso., Yo., K.2 tog., K.3, Yo., K.1B., Yo., K.3, Sl.1, K.1, psso., Yo., * rep. 3 times more from * to *, K.1B., Yo., K.2 tog., P.3.

59th row.—P.3, Sl.1, K.1, psso., Yo., * K.1B., Yo., K.2 tog., K.9, Sl.1, K.1, psso., Yo., Sl.1, K.1, psso., K.3, K.2 tog., Yo., K.2 tog., K.9, Sl.1, K.1, psso., Yo., * rep. 3 times more from * to *, K.1B., Yo., K.2 tog., P.3.

61st row.—P.3, Sl.1, K.1, psso., Yo., * K.1B., Yo., K.2 tog., K.9, Sl.1, K.1, psso., Yo., Sl.1, K.1, psso., K.1, K.2 tog., Yo., K.2 tog., K.9, Sl.1, K.1, psso., Yo., * rep. 3 times more from * to *, K.1B., Yo., K.2 tog., P.3.

63rd row.—P.3, Sl.1, K.1, psso., Yo., * K.1B., Yo., K.2 tog., K.9, Sl.1, K.1, psso., Yo., Sl.1, K.2 tog., psso., Yo., K.2 tog., K.9, Sl.1, K.1, psso., Yo., * rep. 3 times more from * to *, K.1B., Yo., K.2 tog., P.3.

After knitting purl row 64 work PART B rows 43 to 63 incl. another 5 times and then proceed with FINISHING of CHAIR BACK.

FINISHING OF CHAIR BACK.

After knitting last row of purl, turn the work so that the right side faces the knitter. Then finish the edge not by casting off but by crocheting off which is more precisely explained in BASIC INSTRUCTIONS.

Take the stitches together in the following order :—
4 sts., 1 d.c., 10 ch., * 3 sts., 1 d.c., 10 ch., 4 sts., 1 d.c., 10 ch., 3 sts., 1 d.c., 10 ch., 4 sts., 1 d.c., 6 ch., 3 sts., 1 d.c., 6 ch., 4 sts., 1 d.c., 10 ch., 3 sts., 1 d.c., 10 ch., 4 sts., 1 d.c., 10 ch., * rep. 3 times more from * to *, 3 sts., 1 d.c., 10 ch., 4 sts., 1 d.c.

Do not break off the thread but work along the side edge by crocheting 2 d.c. into the loop between the rib formed by the garter stitch used along the 2 selvedge edges. Then turn the corner with 3 d.c. and work along the cast-on edge making 1 d.c. into each cast-on stitch. Now turn the second corner and work the second side edge to give the lace a firmer finish. Finish by making a slip stitch into first d.c. of bottom edge, break off the thread and secure invisibly.

STRETCHING OF CHAIR SET AND SETTEE BACK

CHAIR BACK

Prepare a paper pattern by drawing a square of 16 ins. Divide one side only into 4 sections 4 ins. apart, starting from the corner. Then draw a second line parallel to the marked line, half an inch further inside (This line gives the depth of the scallop).

ARM REST

Draw a square of 12 ins. Divide one side only into 3 sections 4 ins. apart, starting from the corner. Then draw a second line parallel to the marked line ½-in. further inside.

SETTEE BACK

Draw an oblong of 32 ins. by 16 ins. Divide one of the long sides into 8 sections 4 ins. apart, starting from the corner. Then draw a second line parallel to the marked line ½-in. further inside.

The pinning out proceeds now in the same manner for all three pieces of lace.

Take the washed and starched lace, pin down the four corners first, taking care, that the scallop edge is placed on to the marked line of the pattern. Then pin down the straight top edge using the row of double crochet to insert the pins, and placing them along the line about one inch apart.

Now work along the scalloped edge, pinning down first the two centre loops of chain on both sides of the mark on the paper. The two loops of 6 chain give the inside point of the scallop, and are taken together on one pin only, placed on to the inner line of the edge half way along each scallop. Now pin out each remaining loop of chain with one pin only.

Since the edge of the CHAIR SET is the same as the lace edging of the CURTAINS the photo-enlargement of the CURTAIN will be helpful for the shaping of the scallops. Finally pin down the 2 straight side edges placing the pins about 1 ins. apart.

Finish the lace by treating according to BASIC INSTRUCTIONS.

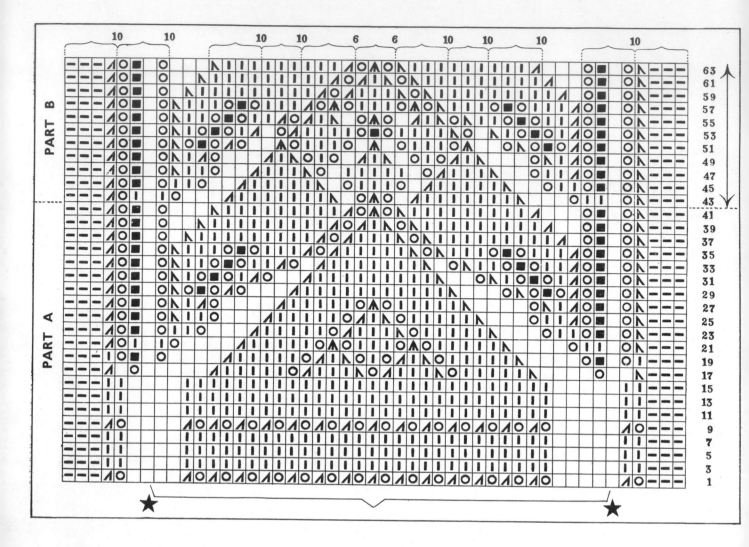

Chart for Chair Set and Settee Back "Rose Leaf"

Every row of which the number is missing, knit purl.

CHAIR BACK:—

Work PART A, PART B 6 times, knitting the section from * to * 4 times in each pattern row.

ARM REST:—

Work PART A, PART B 4 times, knitting the section from * to * 3 times in each pattern row.

SETTEE BACK:—

Work PART A, PART B 6 times, knitting the section from * to * 8 times in each pattern row.

Arm Rests

Commence by casting on **94** stitches and then follow the instructions for CHAIR BACK.

PARTS A and B are worked the same as given in the pattern, but the section from * to * in each pattern row has to be knitted only **3** times. PART B, rows **43** to **63** will have to be worked **4** times altogether and not **6** times as for CHAIR BACK. Then see FINISHING OF CHAIR BACK where the repetition of the section between the asterisks is one less than stated in the pattern.

Settee Back

Commence by casting on **234** stitches, and then knit according to instructions for CHAIR BACK.

PARTS A and B are worked the same only the section from * to * in each pattern row is knitted **8** times instead of **4** times.

This also applies to the FINISHING OF THE LACE.

Adaptation of Pattern

The pattern is composed of 2 Side Edges and the Middle Section. Each Side Edge needs **5** sts. for the start. The Middle Section, which measures **4** ins. in width, can be repeated as many times as one wishes, and requires **28** cast-on stitches. Thus it is possible to produce a lace in any measurement divisible by 4, by casting on as many times **28** sts. as wanted, remembering the extra **10** sts. for the two borders.

In the instructions the Middle Section is referred to as the section from * to *.

The length of the lace can be altered by the different number of repetitions of PART B. One repeat measures about **2** ins.

"Rose Leaf" Design

Curtains

MATERIALS:—

Two SMALL PANELS—5 balls of Crochet Cotton No. 60.
One LARGE PANEL—5 balls of Crochet Cotton No. 60.
2 knitting pins No. 13, length 14 ins.
One steel crochet hook No. 4 to 5.

MEASUREMENTS:—

SMALL PANEL—24 ins. wide, 36 ins. long.
LARGE PANEL—48 ins. wide, 36 ins. long.
The pattern can easily be adapted to other measurements.

Curtain—24 by 36 ins.

CASTING-ON:—

Commence by knitting on 172 stitches, (a loose, loopy selvedge is desired), turn and knit first row of PICOT HEM. Every row of which the number is missing, work purl.

PICOT HEM:—

1st row.—P.3, knit to last three stitches, P.3.

3rd row, 5th row and 7th row.—as 1st row.

9th row.—P.3, K.2 tog., (Yo., Sl.1, K.2 tog., psso.), to be worked to the last 5 stitches, Yo., Sl.1, K.1, psso., P.3. Notice next row is a pattern row.

10th row.—P.4, (M.2 into Yo. of previous row, P.1) to be worked to last three stitches, P.3.

11th row, 13th row, 15th row and 17th row.—as 1st row.

19th row.—This is the row when the PICOT HEM is made.

With an extra needle (possibly a finer one), take up all stitches of the cast-on edge. Then fold the knitting along the little holes and place the extra needle against the purl side of your work. Now knit together the stitches upon the two needles all along the row, taking together one stitch from the needle and one stitch from the cast-on edge.

The double hem thus formed is used for the curtain wire.

If the method explained above appears too difficult, knit row 19 plain, proceed with pattern as follows, and stitch up the hem after the curtain is finished.

21st row.—as 9th row.

22nd row.—as 10th row.

23rd, 25th row, and 27th row.—as 1st row.

29th row.—as 9th row.

30th row.—as 10th row.

31st row, 33rd row, and 35th row.—as 1st row. Now proceed with PART A.

PART A.

37th row.—P.3, Sl.1, K.1, psso., Yo., * (K.3, Yo.) twice, (Sl.1, K.2 tog., psso., Yo., K.3, Yo.) 3 times, K.3, * rep. 5 times more from * to *, Yo., K.2 tog., P.3.

39th row.—P.3, Sl.1, K.1, psso., Yo., * K.2, Sl.1, K.1, psso., (Yo., Sl.1, K.2 tog., psso., Yo., K.3) 3 times, Yo., Sl.1, K.2 tog., psso., Yo., K.2 tog., K.2, * rep. 5 times more from * to *, Yo., K.2 tog., P.3.

After the usual row purl work PART A, rows 37 and 39 another 55 times which brings the rows up to 259. Then proceed with PART B.

PART B.

261st row.—P.3, Sl.1, K.1, psso., Yo., * (K.3, Yo.) twice, (Sl.1, K.2 tog., psso., Yo., K.3, Yo.) 3 times, K.3, * rep. 5 times more from * to *, Yo., K.2 tog., P.3.

263rd row.—P.3, Sl.1, K.1, psso., * Yo., Sl.1, K.1, psso., K.2, (Yo., Sl.1, K.2 tog., psso., Yo., K.3) 3 times, Yo., Sl.1, K.2 tog., psso., Yo., K.2, K.2 tog., * rep. 5 times more from * to *, Yo., K.2 tog., P.3.

265th row.—P.3, K.1, * Yo., K.1, Yo., Sl.1, K.1, psso., K.2, Yo., Sl.1, K.1, psso., (Yo., Sl.1, K.2 tog., psso., Yo., K.3,) twice, Yo., Sl.1, K.2 tog., psso., Yo., K.2 tog., Yo., K.2, K.2 tog., * rep. 5 times more from * to *, Yo., K.1, Yo., K.1, P.3.

267th row.—P.3, K.1, Yo., * Sl.1, K.2 tog., psso., Yo., Sl.1, K.1, psso., K.2, (Yo., Sl.1, K.1, psso.) twice, Yo., Sl.1, K.2 tog., psso., Yo., K.3, Yo., Sl.1, K.2 tog., psso., (Yo., K.2 tog.) twice, Yo., K.2, K.2 tog., Yo., * rep. 5 times more from * to *, Sl.1, K.2 tog., psso., Yo., K.1, P.3.

269th row.—P.3, Sl.1, K.1, psso., Yo., * K.2, Yo., Sl.1, K.1, psso., K.2, (Yo., Sl.1, K.1, psso.) 3 times, Yo., Sl.1, K.2 tog., psso., (Yo., K.2 tog.) 3 times, Yo., K.2, K.2 tog., Yo., K.1, * rep. 5 times more from * to *, K.1, Yo., K.2 tog., P.3.

271st row.—P.3, Sl.1, K.1, psso., Yo., * K.1B., Yo., K.2, Yo., Sl.1, K.1, psso., K.2, (Yo., Sl.1, K.1, psso.) 3 times, K.1, (K.2 tog., Yo.) 3 times, K.2, K.2 tog., Yo., K.2, Yo., * rep. 5 times more from * to *, K.1B., Yo., K.2 tog., P.3.

273rd row.—P.3, Sl.1, K.1, psso., Yo., * K.1B., Yo., K.2 tog., K.2, Yo., Sl.1, K.1, psso., K.2, (Yo., Sl.1, K.1, psso.) twice, Yo., Sl.1, K.2 tog., psso., (Yo., K.2 tog.,) twice, Yo., K.2, K.2 tog., Yo., K.2, Sl.1, K.1, psso., Yo., * rep. 5 times more from * to *, K.1B., Yo., K.2 tog., P.3.

275th row.—P.3, Sl.1, K.1, psso., Yo., * K.1B., Yo., K.2 tog., K.1, Sl.1, K.1, psso., Yo., Sl.1, K.1, psso., K.2, (Yo., Sl.1, K.1, psso.) twice, K.1, (K.2 tog., Yo.) twice, K.2, K.2 tog., Yo., K.2 tog., K.1, Sl.1, K.1, psso., Yo., * rep. 5 times more from * to *, K.1B., Yo., K.2 tog., P.3.

277th row.—P.3, Sl.1, K.1, psso., Yo., * K.1B., Yo., K.2 tog., Yo., K.1B., Yo., Sl.1, K.1, psso., Yo., Sl.1, K.1, psso., K.2, Yo., Sl.1, K.1, psso., Yo., Sl.1, K.2 tog., psso., Yo., K.2 tog., Yo., K.2, K.2 tog., Yo., K.2 tog., Yo., K.1B., Yo., Sl.1, K.1, psso., Yo., * rep. 5 times more from * to *, K.1B., Yo., K.2 tog., P.3.

"Rose Leaf" Design
Curtains

279th row.—P.3, Sl.1, K.1, psso., Yo., * K.1B., Yo., K.2 tog., K.1, Yo., K.1B., Yo., K.1, Sl.1, K.1, psso., Yo., Sl.1, K.1, psso., K.2, Yo., Sl.1, K.1, psso., K.1, K.2 tog., Yo., K.2, K.2 tog., Yo., K.2 tog., K.1, Yo., K.1B., Yo., K.1, Sl.1, K.1, psso., Yo., * rep. 5 times more from * to *, K.1B., Yo., K.2 tog., P.3.

281st row.—P.3, Sl.1, K.1, psso., Yo., * K.1B., Yo., K.2 tog., K.2, Yo., K.1B., Yo., K.2, Sl.1, K.1, psso., Yo., Sl.1, K.1, psso., K.2, Yo., Sl.1, K.2 tog., psso., Yo., K.2, K.2 tog., Yo., K.2 tog., K.2, Yo., K.1B., Yo., K.2, Sl.1, K.1, psso., Yo., * rep. 5 times more from * to *, K.1B., Yo., K.2 tog., P.3.

283rd row.—P.3, Sl.1, K.1, psso., Yo., * K.1B., Yo., K.2 tog., K.3, Yo., K.1B., Yo., K.3, Sl.1, K.1, psso., Yo., Sl.1, K.1, psso., K.5, K.2 tog., Yo., K.2 tog., K.3, Yo., K.1B., Yo., K.3, Sl.1, K.1, psso., Yo., * rep. 5 times more from * to *, K.1B., Yo., K.2 tog., P.3.

285th row.—P.3, Sl.1, K.1, psso., Yo., * K.1B., Yo., K.2 tog., K.9, Sl.1, K.1, psso., Yo., Sl.1, K.1, psso., K.3, K.2 tog., Yo., K.2 tog., K.9, Sl.1, K.1, psso., Yo., * rep. 5 times more from * to *, K.1B., Yo., K.2 tog., P.3.

287th row.—P.3, Sl.1, K.1, psso., Yo., * K.1B., Yo., K.2 tog., K.9, Sl.1, K.1, psso., Yo., Sl.1, K.1, psso., K.1, K.2 tog., Yo., K.2 tog., K.9, Sl.1, K.1, psso., Yo., * rep. 5 times more from * to *, K.1B., Yo., K.2 tog., P.3.

289th row.—P.3, Sl.1, K.1, psso., Yo., * K.1B., Yo., K.2 tog., K.9, Sl.1, K.1, psso., Yo., Sl.1, K.2 tog., psso., Yo., K.2 tog., K.9, Sl.1, K.1, psso., Yo., * rep. 5 times more from * to *, K.1B., Yo., K.2 tog., P.3. Proceed with PART C.

PART C.

291st row.—P.3, Sl.1, K.1, psso., Yo., * K.2, Yo., Sl.1, K.1, psso., K.7, K.2 tog., Yo., Sl.1, K.2 tog., psso., Yo., Sl.1, K.1, psso., K.7, K.2 tog., Yo., K.1, * rep. 5 times more from * to *, K.1, Yo., K.2 tog., P.3.

293rd row.—P.3, Sl.1, K.1, psso., Yo., * K.1B., Yo., K.2, Yo., Sl.1, K.1, psso., K.5, K.2 tog., Yo., K.3, Yo., Sl.1, K.1, psso., K.5, K.2 tog., Yo., K.2, Yo., * rep. 5 times more from * to *, K.1B., Yo., K.2, tog., P.3.

295th row.—P.3, Sl.1, K.1, psso., Yo., * K.1B., Yo., K.2 tog., K.2, Yo., Sl.1, K.1, psso., K.3, K.2 tog., Yo., K.5, Yo., Sl.1, K.1, psso., K.3, K.2 tog., Yo., K.2, Sl.1, K.1, psso., Yo., * rep. 5 times more from * to *, K.1B., Yo., K.2 tog., P.3.

297th row.—P.3, Sl.1, K.1, psso., Yo., * K.1B., Yo., K.2 tog., K.1, Sl.1, K.1, psso., Yo., (Sl.1, K.1, psso., K.1, K.2 tog., Yo., K.1, Yo.) twice, Sl.1, K.1, psso., K.1, K.2 tog., Yo., K.2 tog., K.1, Sl.1, K.1, psso., Yo., * rep. 5 times more from * to *, K.1B., Yo., K.2 tog., P.3.

299th row.—P.3, Sl.1, K.1, psso., Yo., * K.1B., Yo., K.2 tog., Yo., K.1B., Yo., Sl.1, K.1, psso., Yo., (Sl.1, K.2 tog., psso., Yo., K.3, Yo.) twice, Sl.1, K.2 tog., psso., Yo., K.2 tog., Yo., K.1B., Yo., Sl.1, K.1, psso., Yo., * rep. 5 times more from * to *, K.1B., Yo., K.2 tog., P.3.

301st row.—P.3, Sl.1, K.1, psso., Yo., * K.1B., Yo., K.2 tog., K.1, Yo., K.1B., Yo., K.1, Sl.1, K.1, psso., Yo., Sl.1, K.1, psso., K.4, Yo., K.1B., Yo., K.4, K.2 tog., Yo., K.2 tog., K.1, Yo., K.1B., Yo., K.1, Sl.1, K.1, psso., Yo., * rep. 5 times more from * to *, K.1B., Yo., K.2 tog., P.3.

303rd row.—P.3, Sl.1, K.1, psso., Yo., * K.1B., Yo., K.2 tog., K.2, Yo., K.1B., Yo., K.2, Sl.1, K.1, psso., Yo., Sl.1, K.1, psso., K.1, K.2 tog., Yo., Sl.1, K.2 tog., psso., Yo., Sl.1, K.1, psso., K.1, K.2 tog., Yo., K.2 tog., K.2, Yo., K.1B., Yo., K.2, Sl.1, K.1, psso., Yo., * rep. 5 times more from * to *, K.1B., Yo., K.2 tog., P.3.

305th row.—P.3, Sl.1, K.1, psso., Yo., * K.1B., Yo., K.2 tog., K.3, Yo., K.1B., Yo., K.3, Sl.1, K.1, psso., Yo., Sl.1, K.2 tog., psso., Yo., K.3, Yo., Sl.1, K.2 tog., psso., Yo., K.2 tog., K.3, Yo., K.1B., Yo., K.3, Sl.1, K.1, psso., Yo., * rep. 5 times more from * to *, K.1B., Yo., K.2 tog., P.3.

307th row.—P.3, Sl.1, K.1, psso., Yo., * K.1B., Yo., K.2 tog., K.9, Sl.1, K.1, psso., Yo., Sl.1, K.1, psso., K.3, K.2 tog., Yo., K.2 tog., K.9, Sl.1, K.1, psso., Yo., * rep. 5 times more from * to *, K.1B., Yo., K.2 tog., P.3.

309th row.—P.3, Sl.1, K.1, psso., Yo., * K.1B., Yo., K.2 tog., K.9, Sl.1, K.1, psso., Yo., Sl.1, K.1, psso., K.1, K.2 tog., Yo., K.2 tog., K.9, Sl.1, K.1, psso., Yo., * rep. 5 times more from * to *, K.1B., Yo., K.2 tog., P.3.

311th row.—P.3, Sl.1, K.1, psso., Yo., * K.1B., Yo., K.2 tog., K.9, Sl.1, K.1, psso., Yo., Sl.1, K.2 tog., psso., Yo., K.2 tog., K.9, Sl.1, K.1, psso., Yo., * rep. 5 times more from * to *, K.1B., Yo., K.2 tog., P.3.

After knitting purl row 312 work PART B rows 291 to 311 incl. another 3 times and then proceed with FINISHING of CURTAINS.

FINISHING OF CURTAINS.

After knitting last row of purl, turn the work so that the right side faces the knitter. Then finish the edge not by casting off but by crocheting off which is more precisely explained in BASIC INSTRUCTIONS.

Take the stitches together in the following order :—

4 sts., 1 d.c., 10 ch., * 3 sts., 1 d.c., 10 ch., 4 sts., 1 d.c., 10 ch., 3 sts., 1 d.c., 10 ch., 4 sts., 1 d.c., 6 ch., 3 sts., 1 d.c., 6 ch., 4 sts., 1 d.c., 10 ch., 3 sts., 1 d.c., 10 ch., 4 sts., 1 d.c., 10 ch., * rep. 5 times more from * to *, 3 sts., 1 d.c., 10 ch., 4 sts., 1 d.c.

Do not break off the thread but work now along the side edge by crocheting 2 d.c. into the loop between the rib formed by the garter stitch used along the 2 selvedge edges.

Crochet neatly round the opening of PICOT HEM which is to be left open for the curtain wire. Finish with a slip stitch at the wrong side of the CURTAIN and break off. Then crochet down the second side edge starting at the PICOT EDGE and finishing with a slip stitch into the first d.c. of the scalloped edge at the bottom of the CURTAIN. Secure threads invisibly.

Curtain—48 by 36 ins.

Cast on **334** sts. and then follow instructions given for smaller curtain. Notice that when working PARTS A and B the section within the asterisks has to be repeated **11** times more and not 5 times more as stated in pattern.

The same applies to the FINISHING OF CURTAIN.

STRETCHING OF CURTAINS

CURTAIN—24 by 36 ins.

Prepare paper pattern by drawing an oblong of 36 ins. by 24 ins. Divide one of the short sides into 6 sections 4 ins. apart, starting at the corner. Then draw a second line parallel to the marked line ½-in. further inside.

CURTAIN—48 by 36 ins.

Draw an oblong 48 ins. by 36 in. Divide one of the long sides into 12 sections 4 ins. apart, starting from the corner. Then draw a second line parallel to the marked line ½-in. further inside.

The actual PINNING OUT proceeds now in the same manner for all curtains.

Take the washed and starched curtain, pin down the 4 corners first, taking care, that the scalloped edge is placed on to the marked line of the pattern. Then pin down the top edge of the PICOT HEM inserting one pin into each picot and placing them in regular spaces along the straight line.

Now work along the scalloped edge, pinning down first the two centre loops of chain on both sides of the mark on the paper. The two loops of 6 chain give the inside point of the scallop and are taken together on one pin only, placed on to the inner line of the edge half way along each scallop. Now pin out each remaining loop of chain with one pin only.

The photo-enlargement will be helpful for shaping the scallop.

Finally pin down the two straight side edges placing the pins about 1 inch apart.

Finish the lace by treating according to BASIC INSTRUCTIONS.

Adaptation of Curtain Design

The pattern is composed of 2 Side Edges and the Middle Section. Each Side Edge needs 5 sts. for the start. The Middle Section which measures 4 ins. in width can be repeated as many times as one wishes and needs 27 cast-on sts. Thus it is possible to produce a lace panel in any measurement divisible by 4, by casting on as many times 27 sts. as wanted, remembering the extra 10 sts. for the two Side Edges.

In the instructions the Middle Section is referred to as the section from * to *.

The length of the CURTAIN can be changed in two different ways. First, by altering the number of repeats of PART A. Two repeats of PART A measure about three quarters of an inch.

Second, by altering the number of repeats of PART B. One repeat of PART B measures about 2 ins.

THE CURTAIN can be given a quite different appearance by knitting PART A more often than stated in the pattern, and using less repeats of PART B, or vice versa.

The PICOT HEM and the FINISHING OF THE CURTAIN is always the same.

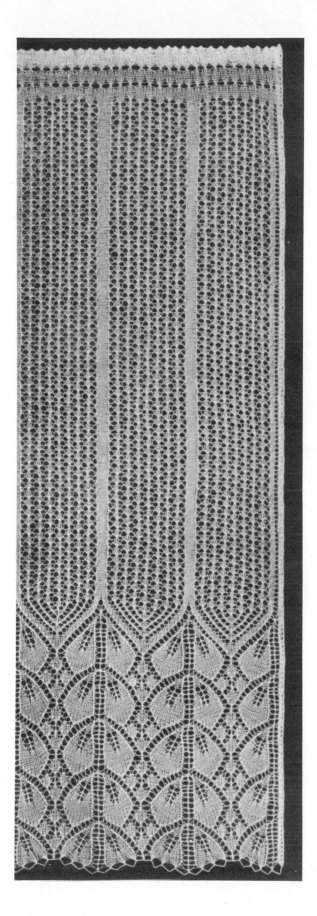

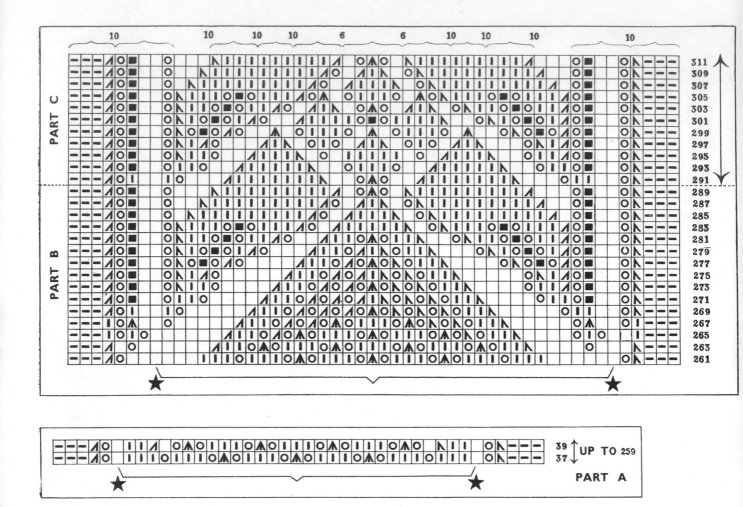

Chart for Curtains "Rose Leaf"

The Casting-on and Picot Hem, see written instructions.

Then follow chart of PART A.

Every row of which the number is missing, work purl.

Work PART A 56 times altogether, PART B once and then PART C 4 times.

Every chart line is one pattern row, but knit the section within the asterisks 6 times when working the Small Panel and 12 times when knitting the Large Panel.

"Candlelight" Design

Bedspread

MATERIALS:—

20 balls of Crochet Cotton No. 40.
2 knitting pins No. 12, length 14 or 15 ins.
One steel crochet hook No. 4.

MEASUREMENTS:—

Length 7 ft., width 5 ft. (Single bed.)
The pattern can easily be adapted to other measurements
as given in ADAPTATION OF PATTERN.

CASTING-ON:—

Commence by casting on 494 stitches, turn and work one row purl. Now knit first pattern row of Bottom Edge.

Notice.—The first and last stitch of every pattern row is slipped knitwise to obtain a chain edge.

ALL stitches are purled in every row of which the number is missing.

BOTTOM EDGE.

1st row.—Sl.1, (Sl.1, K.1, psso., Yo.) 3 times, (K.2 tog., Yo.) to be worked to the last 3 stitches, K.2 tog., Sl.1.

3rd row.—Sl.1, (Sl.1. K.1, psso., Yo.) twice, knit plain to the last 5 stitches, (Yo., K.2 tog.) twice, Sl.1.

5th row, 7th row, 9th row and 11th row.—As 3rd row.

Proceed with PART A.

PART A.

13th row.—Sl.1, (Sl.1, K.1, psso., Yo.) twice, K.1, (Yo., K.2 tog.) to be worked to the last stitch, Sl.1.

15th row.—Sl.1, (Sl.1, K.1, psso., Yo.) twice, knit plain to the last 5 stitches, (Yo., K.2 tog.) twice, Sl.1.

In each of the following pattern rows knit the section from * to * 12 times.

17th row.—Sl.1, (Sl.1, K.1, psso., Yo.) twice, K.1, * (K.2, K.2 tog., Yo., K.1B., Yo., Sl.1, K.1, psso., K.1) 5 times, * K.2, (Yo., K.2 tog.) twice, Sl.1.

19th row.—Sl.1, (Sl.1, K.1, psso., Yo.) twice, K.1, * K.1, K.2 tog., (Yo., Sl.1, K.2 tog., psso., Yo., Sl.1, K.1, psso., K.1, K.2 tog.) twice, Yo., K.3, Yo., (Sl.1, K.1, psso., K.1, K.2 tog., Yo., Sl.1, K.2 tog., psso., Yo.) twice, Sl.1, K.1, psso., * K.2, (Yo., K.2 tog.) twice, Sl.1.

Proceed with PART B.

PART B.

In every row knit the section from * to * 12 times.

21st row.—Sl.1, (Sl.1, K.1, psso., Yo.) twice, * (Sl.1, K.2 tog., psso., Yo., K.3, Yo.) twice, Sl.1, K.2 tog., psso., Yo., K.2 tog., Yo., K.1B., Yo., Sl.1, K.1, psso., Yo., (Sl.1, K.2 tog., psso., Yo., K.3, Yo.) twice, * Sl.1, K.2 tog., psso., (Yo., K.2 tog.) twice, Sl.1.

23rd row.—Sl.1, (Sl.1, K.1, psso., Yo.) twice, * K.1B., Yo., K.5, Yo., K.1B., Yo., K.4, (K.2 tog., Yo.) twice, K.1, M.2, K.1, (Yo., Sl.1, K.1, psso.) twice, K.4, Yo., K.1B., Yo., K.5, Yo., * K.1B., (Yo., K.2 tog.) twice, Sl.1.

25th row.—Sl.1, K.1, Yo., K.2 tog., Yo., * (Sl.1, K.2 tog., psso., Yo., Sl.1, K.1, psso., K.1, K.2 tog., Yo.) twice, K.2 tog., Yo., K.2, Yo., (K.1, o.1), Yo., K.2, (Yo., Sl.1, K.1, psso.) twice, K.1, K.2 tog., Yo., Sl.1, K.2 tog., psso., Yo., Sl.1, K.1, psso., K.1, K.2 tog., Yo., * Sl.1. K.2 tog., psso., Yo., Sl.1. K.1, psso., Yo., K.1, Sl.1.

27th row.—Sl.1, K.1, Yo., K.2 tog., Yo., K.1, * K.2, Yo., Sl.1, K.2 tog., psso., Yo., K.3, Yo., Sl.1, K.2 tog., psso., Yo., K.2 tog., Yo., K.3, Yo., (K.1 o.1) twice, Yo., K.3, Yo., Sl.1, K.1, psso., Yo., Sl.1, K.2 tog., psso., Yo., K.3, Yo., Sl.1, K.2 tog., psso., Yo., K.1, * K.2, Yo., Sl.1, K.1, psso., Yo., K.1, Sl.1.

29th row.—Sl.1, K.1, Yo., K.2 tog., Yo., K.2, * K.3, Yo., K.1B., Yo., K.4, (K.2 tog., Yo.) twice, K.4, Yo., (K.1 o.1) 3 times, Yo., K.4, (Yo., Sl.1, K.1, psso.) twice, K.4, Yo., K.1B., Yo., K.2, * K.3, Yo., Sl.1, K.1, psso., Yo., K.1, Sl.1.

31st row.—Sl.1, K.1, Yo., K.2 tog., Yo., K.1, Yo., Sl.1, K.1, psso., * K.1, K.2 tog., Yo., Sl.1, K.2 tog., psso., Yo., Sl.1, K.1, psso., K.1, (K.2 tog., Yo.) twice, K.5, Yo., (K.1 o.1) 4 times, Yo., K.5, (Yo., Sl.1, K.1, psso.) twice, K.1, K.2 tog., Yo., Sl.1, K.2 tog., psso., Yo., Sl.1, K.1, psso., * K.1, K.2 tog., Yo., K.1, Yo., Sl.1, K.1, psso., Yo., K.1, Sl.1.

33rd row.—Sl.1, K.1, Yo., K.2 tog., Yo., K.3, Yo., * Sl.1, K.2 tog. psso., Yo., K.3, Yo., Sl.1, K.2 tog., psso., Yo., K.2 tog., Yo., K.6, Yo., (K.1 o.1) 5 times, Yo., K.6, Yo., Sl.1, K.1, psso., Yo., Sl.1, K.2 tog., psso., Yo., K.3, Yo., * Sl.1, K. 2 tog., psso., Yo., K.3, Yo., Sl.1, K.1, psso., Yo., K.1, Sl.1.

35th row.—Sl.1, K.1, Yo., K.2 tog., Yo., K.5, Yo., * K.1B., Yo., K.4, (K.2 tog., Yo.)` twice, K.7, Yo., Sl.1, K.1, psso., (K.1 o.1) 4 times, K.2 tog., Yo., K.7, (Yo., Sl.1, K.1, psso.) twice, K.4, Yo., * K.1B., Yo., K.5, Yo., Sl.1, K.1, psso., Yo., K.1, Sl.1.

37th row.—Sl.1, (Sl.1, K.1, psso., Yo.) twice, Sl.1, K.1, psso., K.1, K.2 tog., Yo., * Sl.1, K.2 tog., psso., Yo., Sl.1, K.1, psso., K.1, (K.2 tog., Yo.) twice K.9, Yo., Sl.1, K.1, psso., (K.1 o.1) 3 times, K.2 tog., Yo., K.9, (Yo., Sl.1, K.1, psso.) twice, K.1, K.2 tog., Yo., * Sl.1, K.2 tog., psso., Yo., Sl.1, K.1, psso., K.1, K.2 tog., (Yo., K.2 tog.) twice, Sl.1.

39th row.—Sl.1, (Sl.1, K.1, psso., Yo.) twice, K.2 tog., psso., Yo., K.1, * K.2, Yo., Sl.1, K.2 tog., psso., (Yo., K.2 tog.) twice, K.9, Yo., Sl.1, K.1, psso., (K.1 o.1) twice, K.2 tog., Yo., K.9, (Sl.1, K.1, psso., Yo.) twice, Sl.1, K.2 tog., psso., Yo., K.1, * K.2, Yo., Sl.1, K.2 tog. psso., (Yo., K.2 tog.) twice, Sl.1.

41st row.—Sl.1, (Sl.1, K.1, psso., Yo.) twice, Sl.1, K.1, psso., K.1, * K.2, (K.2 tog., Yo.) twice, K.2 tog., K.10, Yo., Sl.1, K.1, psso., (K.1 o.1), K.2 tog., Yo., K.10, Sl.1, K.1, psso., (Yo., Sl.1, K.1, psso.) twice, K.1, * K.2, K.2 tog., (Yo., K.2 tog.) twice, Sl.1.

43rd row.—Sl.1, (Sl.1, K.1, psso., Yo.) twice, Sl.1, K.1, psso., * K.1, (K.2 tog., Yo.) twice, K.1B., Yo., Sl.1, K.1, psso., K.10, Yo., Sl.2, K.2 tog., p2sso., Yo., K.10, K.2 tog., Yo., K.1B., (Yo., Sl.1, K.1, psso.) twice, * K.1, K.2 tog., (Yo., K.2 tog.) twice, Sl.1.

45th row.—Sl.1, (Sl.1, K.1, psso., Yo.) twice, * Sl.1, K.2 tog., psso., Yo., K.2 tog., Yo., Sl.1, K.2 tog., psso., Yo., Sl.1, K.1, psso., K.21, K.2 tog., Yo., Sl.1, K.2 tog., psso., Yo., Sl.1, K.1, psso., Yo., * Sl.1, K.2 tog., psso., (Yo., K.2 tog.) twice, Sl.1.

47th row.—Sl.1, Sl.1, K.1, psso., Yo., Sl.1, K.1, psso., * K.1, K.2 tog., Yo., K.3, Yo., Sl.1, K.1, psso., K.19, K.2 tog., Yo., K.3, Yo., Sl.1, K.1, psso., * K.1, K.2 tog., Yo., K.2 tog., Sl.1.

49th row.—Sl.1, K.1, Yo., K.1B., Yo., * Sl.1, K.2 tog., psso., Yo., K.5, Yo., Sl.1, K.1, psso., K.17, K.2 tog., Yo., K.5, Yo., * Sl.1, K.2 tog., psso., Yo., K.1B., Yo., K.1, Sl.1.

51st row.—Sl.1, K.1, Yo., K.2 tog., Yo., * Sl.1, K.2 tog., psso., Yo., Sl.1, K.1, psso., K.1, K.2 tog., Yo., K.1, Yo., Sl.1, K.1, psso., K.15, K.2 tog., Yo., K.1, Yo., Sl.1, K.1, psso., K.1, K.2 tog., Yo., * Sl.1, K.2 tog., psso., Yo., Sl.1, K.1, psso., Yo., K.1, Sl.1.

53rd row.—Sl.1, K.1, Yo., K.2 tog., Yo., K.1, * K.2 ,Yo., Sl.1, K.2 tog., psso., Yo., K.3, Yo., Sl.1, K.1, psso., K,13, K.2 tog., Yo., K.3, Yo., Sl.1, K.2 tog., psso., Yo., K.1. * K.2, Yo., Sl.1, K.1, psso., Yo., K.1, Sl.1.

55th row.—Sl.1, K.1, Yo., K.2 tog., Yo., K.2, * K.3, Yo., K.1B., Yo., K.5, Yo., Sl.1, K.1, psso., K.11, K.2 tog., Yo., K.5, Yo., K.1B., Yo., K.2, * K.3, Sl.1, K.1, psso., Yo., K.1, Sl.1.

57th row.—Sl.1, K.1, Yo., K.2 tog., Yo., K.1, Yo., Sl.1, K.1, psso., * K.1, K.2 tog., Yo., Sl.1, K.2 tog., psso., Yo., Sl.1, K.1, psso., K.1, K.2 tog., Yo., K.1, Yo., Sl.1, K.1, psso., K.9, K.2 tog., Yo., K.1, Yo., Sl.1, K.1, psso., K.1, K.2 tog., Yo., Sl.1, K.2 tog., psso., Yo., Sl.1, K.1, psso., * K.1, K.2 tog., Yo., K.1, Yo., Sl.1, K.1, psso., Yo., K.1, Sl.1.

59th row.—Sl.1, K.1, Yo., K.2 tog., Yo., K.3, Yo., *(Sl.1, K.2 tog., psso., Yo., K.3, Yo.) twice, Sl.1, K.1, psso., K.7, K.2 tog., Yo., K.3, Yo., Sl.1, K.2 tog., psso., Yo., K.3, Yo., * Sl.1, K.2 tog., psso., Yo., K.3, Yo., Sl.1, K.1, psso., Yo., K.1, Sl.1.

61st row.—Sl.1, K.1, Yo., K.2 tog., Yo., K.5, Yo., * (K.1B,. Yo., K.5, Yo.) twice, Sl.1, K.1, psso., K.5, K.2 tog., Yo., K.5, Yo., K.1B., Yo., K.5, Yo., * K.1B., Yo., K.5, Yo., Sl.1, K.1, psso., Yo., K.1, Sl.1.

63rd row.—Sl.1, (Sl.1, K.1, psso., Yo.) twice, Sl.1, K.1, psso., K.1, K.2 tog., Yo., * (K.2 tog., psso., Yo., Sl.1, K.1, psso., K.1, K.2 tog., Yo.) twice, K.1, Yo., Sl.1, K.1, psso., K.3, K.2 tog., Yo., K.1, Yo., Sl.1, K.1, psso., K.1, K.2 tog., Yo., Sl.1, K.2 tog., psso., Yo., Sl.1, K.1, psso., K.1, K.2 tog., Yo., * Sl.1, K.2 tog., psso., Yo., Sl.1, K.1, psso., K.1, K.2 tog., (Yo., K.2 tog.) twice, Sl.1.

65th row.—Sl.1, (Sl.1, K.1, psso., Yo.) twice, Sl.1, K.2 tog., psso., Yo., K.1, * K.2, Yo., (Sl.1, K.2 tog., psso., Yo., K.3, Yo.) twice, Sl.1, K.1, psso., K.1, K.2 tog., (Yo., K.3, Yo., Sl.1, K.2 tog., psso.) twice, Yo., K.1, * K.2, Yo., Sl.1, K.2 tog., psso., (Yo., K.2 tog.) twice, Sl.1.

67th row.—Sl.1, (Sl.1, K.1, psso., Yo.) twice, Sl.1, K.1, psso., K.1, * K.3, (Yo., K.1B., Yo., K.5) twice, Yo., Sl.1, K.2 tog., psso., (Yo., K.5, Yo., K.1B.) twice, Yo., K.2, * K.2, K.2 tog., (Yo., K.2 tog.) twice, Sl.1.

69th row.—Sl.1, (Sl.1, K.1, psso., Yo.) twice, Sl.1, K.1, psso., * K.1, K.2 tog., (Yo., Sl.1, K.2 tog., psso., Yo., Sl.1, K.1, psso., K.1, K.2 tog.) twice, Yo., K.3, Yo., (Sl.1, K.1, psso., K.1, K.2 tog., Yo., Sl.1, K.2 tog., psso., Yo.) twice, Sl.1, K.1, psso., * K.1, K.2 tog., (Yo., K.2 tog.) twice, Sl.1.

Now work PART B rows 21 to 69 incl. another 17 times, and then proceed with PART C.

PART C.

In every row knit the section from * to * 12 times.

71st row.—Sl.1, (Sl.1, K.1, psso., Yo.) twice, * (Sl.1, K.2 tog., psso., Yo., K.3, Yo.) twice, Sl.1, K.2 tog., psso., Yo., K.5, Yo., (Sl.1, K.2 tog., psso., Yo., K.3, Yo.) twice, * Sl.1, K.2 tog., psso., (Yo., K.2 tog.) twice, Sl.1.

73rd row.—Sl.1, (Sl.1, K.1, psso., Yo.) twice, * (K.1B., Yo., K.5, Yo.) twice, K.1B., Yo., K.2 tog., K.3, Sl.1, K.1, psso., Yo., (K.1B., Yo., K.5, Yo.) twice, * K.1B., (Yo., K.2 tog.) twice, Sl.1.

75th row.—Sl.1, (Sl.1, K.1, psso., Yo.) twice, knit plain to the last 5 stitches, (Yo., K.2 tog.) twice, Sl.1.

77th row.—Sl.1, (Sl.1, K.1, psso., Yo.) twice, (K.2 tog., Yo.) to be worked to the last 6 stitches, K.1, (Yo., K.2 tog.) twice, Sl.1. Now proceed with TOP EDGE.

TOP EDGE.

79th row, 81st row, 83rd row, 85th row and 87th row.—As 3rd row of BOTTOM EDGE.

89th row.—Sl.1, (Sl.1, K.1, psso., Yo.) twice, (K.2 tog., Yo.) to be worked to the last 6 stitches, K.1, (Yo., K.2 tog.) twice, Sl.1.

90th row.—Work purl.

FINISHING OF BEDSPREAD

After last row cast off all stitches fairly loosely so that the edge stretches easily to the necessary measurements. At the end of row do not break off the thread but work all round the cloth one row of double crochet to give the lace a firmer finish. Work along the SIDE EDGES at least 2 d.c. into each slip stitch and along the BOTTOM and TOP EDGE one d.c. into each stitch.

STRETCHING OF BEDSPREAD

The finished cover can be made ready for use in two different ways.

1. Wash and starch the lace cloth and stretch it gently into shape lying flat on a large sheet. When almost dry iron carefully pulling the lace at the same time to its correct measurements.

2. An even more satisfactory result will be obtained by preparing a paper pattern drawing an oblong 84 by 60 ins. Mark 36 points along the two long sides, about 2¼ ins. apart, starting at the corners. Take the washed and starched cover, place in position, and fix the four corners first. Then pin down the Bottom and Top Edges using the firm row of d.c. to insert the pins, about 1 in. apart along the line.

Now pin out the points of the zigzag border placing them, with one pin only on to the marks on the paper pattern.

Finish by treating the lace according to BASIC INSTRUCTIONS.

Chart for Bedspread "Candlelight"

CASTING ON and BOTTOM EDGE row 1 to 11 incl. see written instruction, then work chart PART A.
Proceed with PART B working rows 21 to 69 incl. 18 times.
Now knit PART C rows 71 to 77 incl. and finish with TOP EDGE rows 79 to 90 as given in written instructions.
Every chart line is one pattern row, but knit the section between the asterisks 12 times.
Every row of which the number is missing work purl.

Adaptation of "Candlelight" Design

The "CANDLELIGHT" design is made up of the ZIGZAG BORDER on each side and the MIDDLE PANEL, the latter being referred to in the pattern as the section between the asterisks. With altering the number of MIDDLE PANELS the width of the bedspread is altered accordingly.

The borders on the right and left measure together about 3 ins., and need 14 sts. for the start. For the knitting of one middle section 40 cast-on stitches are required, and its measurement is between 1½ to 5 ins. in width. It is therefore possible to cast on as many times 40 stitches as the width of the cover requires, remembering that an **extra 14** stitches have to be added for the two borders measuring 3 ins.

The length of the pattern is governed by the repetition of PART B, one repeat measures about 4½ ins.

Whatever the size of the bedspread the parts repeat in the same order as given in the pattern, and only the repetition of the section from * to *, and the repeat of PART B will alter according to your adjustments.

If a cover for a Double-bed is required and the 15 ins. knitting pins should prove to be too short, it is possible to use, instead of two knitting pins, two circular knitting needles of the same number, length 30 to 36 ins. The long points of the circular needles would then be used for knitting the stitches, and on to the shorter points push pieces of cork to prevent the stitches from slipping off the ends.

CHAPTER III

WORKING INSTRUCTIONS
FOR DESIGNS IN ROUND KNITTING

"Coronet" Design

Doily

MATERIALS:—

One ball of Crochet Cotton No. 50 is sufficient for 4 doilies. Four double pointed knitting needles No. 13, length 7 ins. One steel crochet hook No. 4 or 5.

MEASUREMENTS:—

10 ins. diameter. This measurement can be increased by about 1½ to 2 ins. by using No. 12 knitting needles.

CASTING ON:—

Commence by casting on (either method) 12 sts. on to three needles having 4 sts. on each needle. Knit 2 rounds plain, then work first pattern round of PART A.

Every round of which the number is missing knit plain.

X in front of pattern round—see ABBREVIATIONS.

PART A.

1st round.—(Yo., K.1B.) 12 times.

2nd round.—(M.3 into Yo. of previous round, K.1) 12 times.

Six rounds plain. Then proceed with PART B.

PART B.

Knit each section from [to] 6 times in one round.

9th round.—[K.2, K.2 tog., Yo.2, Sl.1, K.1, psso., K.2] Notice that next round is a pattern round.

10th round.—[K.3, M.6 into Yo.2 of previous round, K.3.] 4 rounds plain.

15th round.—[K.12, Yo.]

17th round.—[K.12, Yo., K.1, Yo.]

19th round.—[K.10, K.2 tog., Yo., K.3, Yo.]

Before knitting the following rounds pay special attention to the working of Yo.2 as explained in BASIC INSTRUCTIONS.

21st round.—[Sl.1, K.1, psso., K.7, K.2 tog., Yo.2, K.2, Yo.2, Sl.1, K.1, psso., K.1, Yo.2.]

23rd round.—[Sl.1, K.1, psso., K.5, K.2 tog., Yo.2, K.1, (K.2 tog., Yo.2. Sl.1. K.1. psso.) twice, K.1, Yo.2.]

25th round.—[Sl.1, K.1, psso., K.3, K.2 tog., Yo.2, K.1, (K.2 tog., Yo.2, Sl.1, K.1, psso.) 3 times, K.1, Yo.2.]

27th round.—[Sl.1, K.1, psso., K.1, K.2 tog., Yo.2, K.1, (K.2 tog., Yo.2, Sl.1, K.1, psso.) 4 times, K.1, Yo.2.]

29th round.—[Sl.1, K.2 tog., psso., Yo.2, K.1, (K.2 tog., Yo.2, Sl.1, K.1, psso.) 5 times, K.1, Yo.2.]

31st round.—[M.2, Yo.2, K.1, (K.2 tog., Yo.2, Sl.1, K.1, psso.) 6 times, K.1, Yo.2.] Proceed with PART C.

PART C

Knit each section from [to] 12 times in one round.

X *33rd round.*—[Yo., K.2, (K.2 tog., Yo.2, Sl.1, K.1, psso.) 3 times, K.2.]

35th round.—[Yo., K.1, Yo., Sl.1, K.1, psso., K.2, (K.2 tog., Yo.2, Sl.1, K.1, psso.) twice, K.2, K.2 tog.]

37th round.—[Yo., K.3, Yo., Sl.1, K.1, psso., K.3, K.2 tog., Yo.2, Sl.1, K.1, psso., K.3, K.2 tog.]

39th round.—[Yo. K.5, Yo., Sl.1, K.1, psso., K.8, K.2 tog.]

41st round.—[Yo., K.2, K.2 tog., Yo.2, K.3. Yo., Sl.1, K.1, psso., K.6, K.2 tog.]

Next round is a pattern round.

42nd round.—[K.4, M.6 into Yo.2 of previous round, K.12.]

43rd round.—[Yo., K.14. Yo., Sl.1, K.1, psso., K.4, K.2 tog.]

45th round.—[Yo., K.16, Yo., Sl.1, K.1, psso., K.2, K.2 tog.]

46th round.—Knit plain and see FINISHING of DOILY.

FINISHING OF DOILY

After knitting plain round 46 finish the doily with a chain of crochet as follows. (3 sts., 1 dc., 9 ch.) 5 times, 3 sts., 1 dc., 6 ch., 4 sts., 1 dc., 6 ch., repeat 11 times. Finish with a slip stitch into the first dc. and break off.

STRETCHING OF DOILY

Prepare paper pattern by drawing a circle of 9 ins. diameter. Mark round the circle 12 points 2⅓ ins. apart. Then draw a second outer circle of 10 ins. diameter thus giving the real size of the doily.

After preparing the lace, pin out the Doily by placing the 2 loops of 6 chain on one pin only on to each point marked round the inner circle. This is the inner point of each scallop. The outer point of the scallop is obtained by pinning down the central loop of chain on to the outer circle in the middle of the scallop. Then pin down each remaining loop of chain, trying to shape the scallops according to the photo.

Finish by treating the lace according to BASIC INSTRUCTIONS.

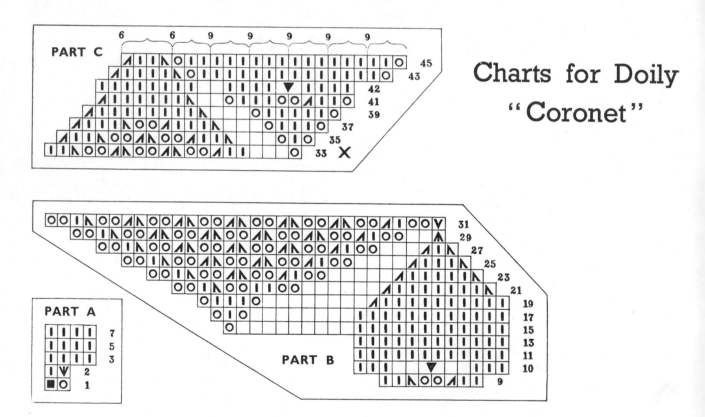

Charts for Doily "Coronet"

PART A:—
Every chart line to be knitted 12 times in one round.

PART B:—
Every chart line to be knitted 6 times in one round.

PART C:—
Every chart line to be knitted 12 times in one round.

NOTICE:—
Every round of which the number is missing knit plain. Pay special attention to rounds 10 and 42.

"Valentine" Design

Cheval Set

MATERIALS:—

One ball of Crochet Cotton No. 50.
Four double pointed knitting needles No. 13, length 7 ins.
One steel crochet hook No. 4 or 5.

MEASUREMENTS:—

LARGE DOILY—12 ins. diameter.
SMALL DOILY—8 ins. diameter.

NOTICE:—

For Large Doily

work casting-on and PARTS A, B, C, and D.

For Small Doily

work casting-on and PARTS A and B.

CASTING ON:—

Commence by casting on (either method) 10 stitches on to 3 needles, having 3 stitches each on the first and second needle, and 4 stitches on the third needle. Knit one round plain, and then work first round of PART A.

Every round of which the number is missing knit plain.

PART A.

1st round.—(Yo., K.1B.) 10 times.
3 rounds plain.
5th round.—(Yo., K.1B.) 20 times.
3 rounds plain.
9th round.—(Yo., K.1B.) 40 times.
7 rounds plain and then proceed with **PART B.**

PART B.

Knit each section from [to] 10 times in one round.

17th round.—[K.7, Yo., K.1, Yo.]

19th round.—[Sl.1, K.1, psso., K.3, K.2 tog., Yo., K.1, M.3, K.1, Yo.]

21st round.—[Sl.1, K.1, psso., K.1, K.2 tog., Yo., K.7, Yo.]

23rd round.—[Sl.1, K.2 tog., psso., Yo., K.4, M.2, K.4, Yo.]

25th round.—[K.1B, Yo., K.12, Yo.]

27th round.—[Yo., K.1B, Yo., K.14.]

29th round.—[Yo., Sl.1, K.2 tog., psso., Yo., Sl.1, K.1, psso., K.10, K.2 tog.]

31st round.—[Yo., K.3, (Yo., Sl.1, K.1, psso., K.2, K.2 tog.) twice.]

33rd round.—[Yo., K.1, Yo., Sl.1, K.2 tog., psso., (Yo., K.1, Yo., Sl.2, K.2 tog., p2sso.) twice.]

35th round.—[(K.3, Yo., K.1B, Yo.) 3 times.]

When working SMALL DOILY of 8 ins. diameter see now FINISHING of SMALL DOILY.

When working LARGE DOILY proceed with following PART C.

PART C.

37th round.—(Sl.1, K.2 tog., psso., Yo.) 60 times.

39th round.—(Yo., K.1B., Yo., K.3) 30 times.

41st round.—(Yo., Sl.1, K.2 tog., psso.) 60 times. Notice next round is a pattern round.

42nd round.—(M.3 into Yo. of previous round, K.1) 60 times.

6 rounds plain. Proceed with PART D.

PART D.

Knit each section from [to] 24 times in one round.

49th round.—[Yo., K.1, Yo., Sl.1, K.1, psso., K.5, K.2 tog.]

51st round.—[Yo., K.3, Yo., Sl.1, K.1, psso., K.3, K.2 tog.]

53rd round.—[Yo., K.1, Yo., Sl.1, K.2 tog., psso., Yo., K.1, Yo., Sl.1, K.1, psso., K.1, K.2 tog.]

55th round.—[K.3, Yo., K.1B., Yo., K.3, Yo., Sl.1, K.2 tog., psso., Yo.]

56th round.—Knit plain. Now see FINISHING OF LARGE DOILY.

FINISHING OF SMALL DOILY.

After knitting last plain round 36 finish the DOILY with a chain of crochet as follows :

(3 sts., 1 d.c., 9 ch.) 3 times, (3 sts., 1 d.c., 7 ch.) twice, 3 sts., 1 d.c., 9 ch. Repeat 9 times.

Finish with a slip stitch into first d.c. and break off. Secure thread invisibly.

FINISHING OF LARGE DOILY.

After knitting last plain round 56 finish the DOILY with a chain of crochet as follows :

(3 sts., 1 d.c., 9 ch.) twice, (3 sts., 1 d.c., 7 ch.) twice. Repeat 23 times.

Finish with a slip stitch into first d.c. and break off. Secure thread invisibly.

STRETCHING OF CHEVAL SET.

Prepare paper pattern for each of the two doilies.

LARGE DOILY.—Draw a circle of 11½ ins. diam. Mark round the circle 24 points, about 1½ ins. apart. Then draw a second outer circle of 12 ins. diam., which gives the size of the doily.

SMALL DOILY.—Draw a circle of 7½ ins. diam. Mark round the circle 10 points about 2⅓ ins. apart. Then draw the second outer circle of 8 ins. diam.

Now pin out the prepared doilies trying to shape the edge according to photo. Put the two loops of 7 ch. on to one pin only placing the same on to the points marked round the inner circle. Then pin out the remaining loops of chain separately along the outer circle.

Finish by treating the lace as directed in BASIC INSTRUCTIONS.

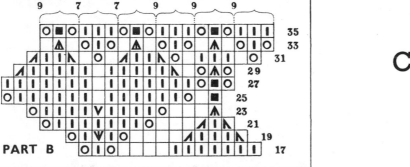

Charts for
Cheval Set
"Valentine"

Large Doily:—Work PARTS A, B, C and D.
Small Doily:—Work PARTS A and B.
PART A and PART B:—Every chart line to be knitted 10 times in one round.
PART C:—Every chart line to be knitted 30 times in one round.
PART D:—Every chart line to be knitted 24 times in one round.
Every round of which the number is missing knit plain.
Notice that sometimes more than one plain round is knitted between the pattern rounds.

"Azalea" Design

Luncheon Set

MATERIALS:—

CENTRE PIECE, PLACE DOILY, PLATE and GLASS DOILY—2 balls of Crochet Cotton No. 40.

Four double pointed knitting needles No. 13, length 7 ins. One steel crochet hook No. 4.

To complete CENTRE PIECE four double pointed knitting needles 9 ins. length, or a circular knitting needle No. 13, length 16 ins. will be required.

MEASUREMENTS:—

CENTRE PIECE.—16 ins. diameter.

PLACE DOILY.—13 ins. diameter.

PLATE DOILY.—10 ins. diameter.

GLASS DOILY.—7 ins. diameter.

Centre Piece

CASTING-ON:—

Commence by casting on (either method) 12 stitches on to 3 needles, having 4 stitches on each needle. Knit 2 rounds plain and work first pattern round of PART A.

Every round of which the number is missing knit plain.

PART A.

Knit each section from [to] 6 times in one round.

1st round.—[(Yo., K.1B.) twice.]
3rd round.—[K.1, M.3, K.2.]
5th round.—[K.2, M.3, K.3.]
7th round.—[K.3, M.3, K.4.]
9th round.—[K.4, M.3, K.5.]
11th round.—[Yo., K.5, M.3, K.5, Yo., K.1B.]
13th round.—[Yo., K.1B., Yo., K.13, (Yo., K.1B.) twice.]

PART B.

Knit each section from [to] 6 times in one round.

Ignore asterisks when working Part B rounds 15 to 25 for the first time.

15th round.—[K.1, * M.3, K.1, Sl.1, K.1, psso., K.9, K.2 tog., K.1, * M.3, K.2.]

17th round.—[K.2, * M.3, K.2, Sl.1, K.1, psso., K.7, K.2 tog., K.2, * M.3, K.3.]

19th round.—[K.3, * M.3, K.3, Sl.1, K.1, psso., K.5, K.2 tog., K.3, * M.3, K.4.]

21st round.—[K.4, * M.3, K.4, Sl.1, K.1, psso., K.3, K.2 tog., K.4, * M.3, K.5.]

23rd round.—[Yo., K.5, * M.3, K.5, Sl.1, K.1, psso., K.1, K.2 tog., K.5, * M.3, K.5, Yo., K.1B.]

25th round.—[Yo., K.1B., Yo., K.6, * K.7, Yo., Sl.1, K.2 tog., psso., Yo., K.6, * K.7, (Yo., K.1B.) twice.]

27th round to 37th round incl. are the same as rounds 15 to 25 but knit the part from * to * twice in each section.

39th round to 49th round incl. are the same as rounds 15 to 25 but knit the part from * to * 3 times in each section.

51st round to 61st round incl. are the same as rounds 15 to 25 but knit the part from * to * 4 times in each section.

62nd round.—Knit plain and then see FINISHING of LUNCHEON SET.

Place Mat

Work according to instructions for CENTRE PIECE up to round 49 incl., knit one round plain and then see FINISHING OF LUNCHEON SET.

Plate Mat

Work according to instructions for CENTRE PIECE up to round 37 incl., knit one round plain, and then see FINISHING OF LUNCHEON SET.

Glass Mat

Work according to instructions for CENTRE PIECE up to round 25 incl., knit one round plain, and then see FINISHING OF LUNCHEON SET.

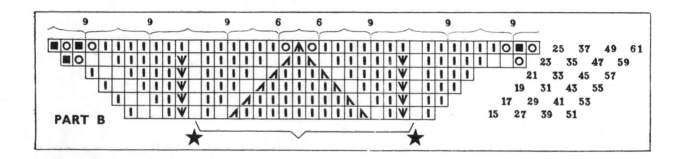

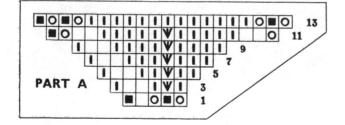

Charts for Luncheon Set "Azalea"

Centre Piece:—
Work PARTS A and B up to round 61 incl.

Place Doily:—
Work PARTS A and B up to round 49 incl.

Plate Doily:—
Work PARTS A and B up to round 37 incl.

Glass Doily:—
Work PARTS A and B up to round 25 incl.

PART A:—
Every chart line to be knitted 6 times in one round.

PART B:—
Every chart line to be knitted 6 times in one round but knit the section from * to * as many times as PART B is repeated. (e.g. when knitting PART B for the first time the section from * to * is worked once. When knitting PART B for the second time the section between the asterisks is worked twice etc.)

Every line of which the number is missing knit plain.

FINISHING OF LUNCHEON SET.

CENTRE PIECE.—After knitting last plain round knit 2 more stitches and then finish the lace doilies with a chain of crochet as follows :—

Work the section from [to] 6 times.

[5 sts., 1 d.c., 9 ch., * 5 sts., 1 d.c., 9 ch., 4 sts., 1 d.c., 6 ch., 3 sts., 1 d.c., 6 ch., 4 sts., 1 d.c., 9 ch., * rep. 3 times more from * to *, (5 sts., 1 d.c., 9 ch.) 3 times.]

Finish with a slip stitch into first d.c. and break off. Secure thread invisibly.

PLACE MAT.—Crochet off as for CENTRE PIECE but work the part from * to * only 3 times.

PLATE MAT.—Crochet off as for CENTRE PIECE but work the part within the asterisks only twice.

GLASS MAT.—Crochet off as for CENTRE PIECE but work the part from * to * only once ignoring asterisks.

STRETCHING OF LUNCHEON SET.

Prepare a paper pattern for each of the four lace mats, which all have a hexagonal shape.

CENTRE PIECE.—Draw a circle 16 ins. diameter. Mark round the circle 6 points at a distance of 8 ins. from each other and join these points by straight lines to form a hexagon.

PLACE DOILY.—Draw a circle 13 ins. diameter. Mark round the circle 6 points 6½ ins. apart and join them by straight lines, thus forming the hexagon.

PLATE DOILY.—Draw a circle 10 ins. diam. Mark round the circle 6 points 5 ins. apart. Complete the hexagon by joining these points.

GLASS DOILY.—Draw a circle 7 ins. diam. Mark round the circle 6 points 3½ ins. apart and complete the hexagon.

Now pin out the lace mats trying to shape the scallops according to photo. The two loops of chain in the centre of the scallop formed by the double leaves are pinned down on both sides of the marked points, thus giving the corners for the hexagon. The other loops are pinned out along the straight line, except for the two loops of 6 chain which are pinned down together by one pin only about ½ in. inside the straight line. Finish by treating the lace as directed in BASIC INSTRUCTIONS.

"Primula Design"

Coffee Cloth

MATERIALS :—

One ball of Crochet Cotton No. 60.

Four double pointed knitting needles No. 12, length 7 ins., one circular knitting needle No. 12, length 24 ins. One steel crochet hook No. 5.

MEASUREMENTS :—

22 ins. diameter.

CASTING-ON :—

Commence by casting on 8 stitches (either method), having 3 stitches each on the first and second needle, and 2 stitches on the third needle. By help of this arrangement 3 sections of one round of PART A will be worked on each of the first two needles, and 2 sections on the third needle. Now knit 2 rounds plain, and then start to work first pattern round of PART A.

Every round of which the number is missing knit plain.

X and XX in front of pattern rounds see Abbreviations.

PART A.

Knit each section from [to] 8 times in one round.

1st round.—[Yo., K.1]

3rd round.—[Yo., K.1, Yo., K.1]
3 rounds plain.

7th round.—[(Yo., K.1) 4 times.]

9th round.—[Yo., K.2 tog., Yo., S1.1, K.2 tog., psso., Yo., S1.1, K.1, psso., Yo., K.1B.]

11th round.—[Yo., K.2 tog., Yo., K.3, Yo., S1.1, K.1, psso., Yo., K.1B.]

13th round.—[(Yo., K.2 tog.) twice, Yo., K.1, (Yo., S1.1, K.1, psso.) twice, Yo., K.1B.]

15th round.—[(Yo., K.2 tog.) twice, Yo., K.3, (Yo., S1.1, K.1, psso.) twice, Yo., K.1B.]

17th round.—[(K.2 tog., Yo.) 3 times, K.1B., (Yo., S1.1, K.1, psso.) 3 times, K.1.]

X *19th round.*—[(Yo., K.2 tog.) twice, (Yo., K.1B.) 3 times, (Yo., S1.1, K.1, psso.) twice, Yo., S1.1, K.2 tog., psso.]

21st round.—[K.2 tog., Yo., K.2 tog., (K.1, Yo., K.1B., Yo.) 3 times, K.1, S1.1, K.1, psso., Yo., S1.1, K.1, psso., K.1.]

X *23rd round.*—[Yo., K.2 tog., K.2, Yo., K.1B., Yo., K.2, Yo., S1.1, K.2 tog., psso., Yo., K.2, Yo., K.1B., Yo., K.2, S1.1, K.1, psso., Yo., S1.1, K.2 tog., psso.]

25th round.—[K.2 tog., K.3, Yo., K.1B., Yo., K.3, Yo., S1.1, K.2 tog., psso., Yo., K.3, Yo., K.1B., Yo., K.3, S1.1, K.1, psso., K.1.]

Now proceed with PART B.

PART B.

Knit each section from [to] 16 times in one round.

X *27th round.* — [K.4, Yo., K.1B., Yo., K.4, Yo., S1.1, K.2 tog., psso., Yo.]

29th round.—[S1.1, K.1, psso., K.2, Yo., K.1, Yo., K.1B., Yo., K.1, Yo., K.2, K.2 tog., Yo., S1.1, K.2 tog., psso., Yo.]

31st round.—[S1.1, K.1, psso., (K.2, Yo.) twice, K.1B., (Yo., K.2) twice, K.2 tog., Yo., S1.1, K.2 tog., psso., Yo.]

33rd round.—[S1.1, K.1, psso., K.2, Yo., K.3, Yo., K.1B., Yo., K.3, Yo., K.2, K.2 tog., Yo., S1.1, K.2 tog., psso., Yo.]

35th round.—[S1.1, K.1, psso., K.2, Yo., K.4, Yo., K.1B., Yo., K.4, Yo., K.2, K.2 tog., Yo., S1.1, K.2 tog., psso., Yo.]

37th round.—[S1.1, K.1, psso., K.2, Yo., S1.1, K.1, psso., K.7, K.2 tog., Yo., K.2, K.2 tog., psso., Yo., S1.1, K.2 tog. psso., Yo.]

39th round.—[S1.1, K.1, psso., K.2, Yo., S1.1, K.1, psso., K.5, K.2 tog., Yo., K.2, K.2 tog., Yo., S1.1, K.2 tog., psso., Yo.]

41st round.—[S1.1, K.1, psso., K.2, Yo., S1.1, K.1, psso., K.3, K.2 tog., Yo., K.2, K.2 tog., Yo., K.3, Yo.]

43rd round.—[S1.1, K.1, psso., K.2, Yo., S1.1, K.1, psso., K.1, K.2 tog., Yo., K.2, K.2 tog., Yo., K.1, Yo., S1.1, K.2 tog., psso., Yo., K.1, Yo.]

45th round.—[S1.1, K.1, psso., K.2, Yo., S1.1, K.2 tog., psso., Yo., K.2, K.2 tog., Yo., K.3, Yo., K.1B., Yo., K.3, Yo.]

47th round.—[S1.1, K.1, psso., K.5, K.2 tog., Yo., K.1, (Yo., S1.1, K.2 tog., psso.) 3 times, Yo., K.1, Yo.]

49th round.—[S1.1, K.1, psso., K.3, K.2 tog., (Yo., K.3, Yo., K.1B.) twice, Yo., K.3, Yo.]

51st round.—[S1.1, K.1, psso., K.1, K.2 tog., Yo., K.1, (Yo., S1.1, K.2 tog., psso.) 5 times, Yo., K.1, Yo.]

53rd round.—[Yo., S1.1, K.2 tog., psso., (Yo., K.3, Yo., K.1B.) 3 times, Yo., K.3.]

Now proceed with PART C.

PART C.

Knit each section from [to] 64 times in one round.

55th round.—[(Yo., S1.1, K.2 tog., psso.) twice.]

57th round.—[K.3, Yo., K.1B., Yo.]

59th round.—[(S1.1, K.2 tog., psso., Yo.) twice.]

61st round.—[Yo., K.1B., Yo., K.3.]

63rd round.—same as round 55.

65th round.—same as round 57.

67th round.—same as round 59.

69th round.—same as round 61.

Now proceed with PART D.

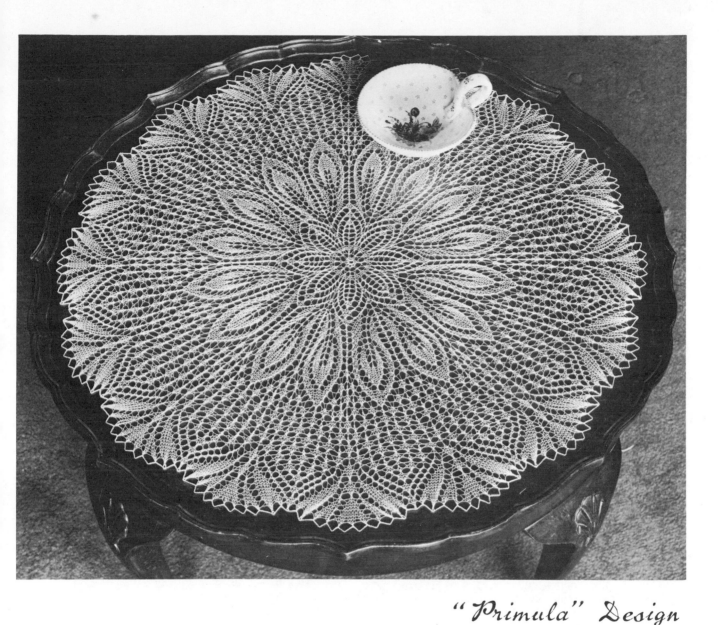

"Primula" Design

PART D.

Knit each section from [to] 16 times in one round.

71st round.—[(Yo., S1.1, K.2 tog., psso.) 4 times, Yo., K.3, (Yo., S1.1, K.2 tog., psso.) 3 times.]

73rd round.—[(K.3, Yo., K.1B., Yo.) twice, K.5, Yo., K.1B., Yo., K.3, Yo., K.1B., Yo.]

75th round.—[(S1.1, K.2 tog., psso., Yo.) 3 times, (K.2 tog., Yo.) twice, S1.1, K.2 tog., psso., (Yo., S1.1, K.1, psso.) twice, (Yo., S1.1, K.2 tog., psso.) twice, Yo.]

77th round.—[Yo., K.1B., Yo., K.3, Yo., K.1B., Yo., K.2 tog., Yo., K.2, Yo., K.3, Yo., K.2, Yo., S1.1, K.1, psso., Yo., K.1B., Yo., K.3.]

79th round.—[(S1.1., K.2 tog., psso., Yo.) twice, (K.2 tog. Yo.) twice, K.3, Yo., K.5, Yo., K.3, (Yo., S1.1, K.1, psso.) twice, Yo., S1.1, K.2 tog., psso., Yo.]

81st round.—[K.1, (K.2 tog., Yo.,) 3 times, K.4, Yo., K.2 tog., Yo., S1.1, K.2 tog., psso., Yo., S1.1, K.1, psso., Yo., K.4, (Yo., S1.1, K.1, psso.) 3 times.]

XX *83rd round.*—[(Yo., K.2, tog.) twice, Yo., K.5, Yo., K.2, Yo., K.3, Yo., K.2, Yo., K.5, (Yo., S1.1, K.1, psso.) twice, Yo., S1.1, K.2 tog., psso.]

85th round.—[(K.2 tog., Yo.) twice, K.6, Yo., K.3, Yo., K.5, Yo., K.3, Yo., K.6, (Yo., S1.1, K.1, psso.) twice K.1.]

X *87th round.*—[Yo., K.2 tog., Yo., K.7, Yo., K.4, Yo., K.7, Yo., K.4, Yo., K.7, Yo., S1.1, K.1, psso., Yo., S1.1, K.2 tog., psso.]

89th round.—[K.2 tog., Yo., K.6, K.2 tog., Yo., K.5, Yo., K.9, Yo., K.5, Yo., S1.1, K.1, psso., K.6, Yo., S1.1, K.1, psso., K.1.]

90th round.—Knit plain.

Now see FINISHING OF CLOTH.

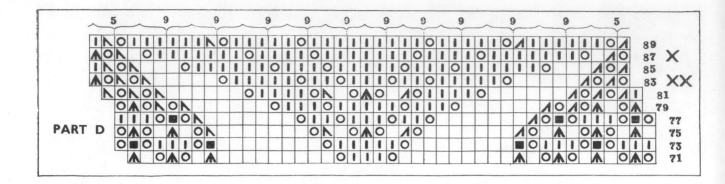

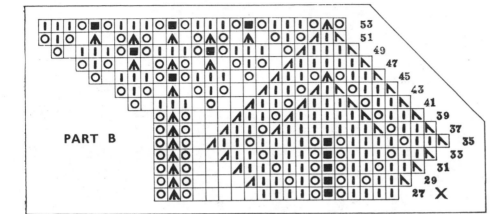

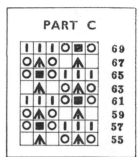

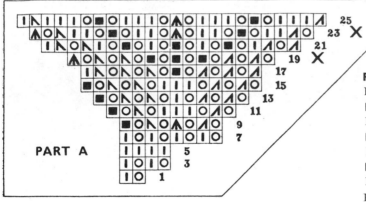

Charts for Coffee Cloth "Primula"

PART A :—
Every chart line to be knitted 8 times in one round.

PART B :—
Every chart line to be knitted 16 times in one round.

PART C :—
Every chart line to be knitted 64 times in one round.

PART D :—
Every chart line to be knitted 16 times in one round.
Every round of which the number is missing knit plain.

FINISHING OF COFFEE CLOTH.

After knitting plain round 90 knit another stitch, and then finish the cloth with a chain of crochet as follows : (4 sts., 1 d.c., 9 ch.) 3 times, (3 sts., 1 d.c., 9 ch.) 5 times, (4 sts., 1 d.c., 9 ch.) twice, 4 sts., 1 d.c., 5 ch., 3 sts., 1 d.c., 5 ch. Repeat 15 times. Finish with a slip stitch and break off.

STRETCHING OF COFFEE CLOTH.

Prepare a paper pattern by drawing a circle of 21 ins. diameter. Mark round the circle 16 points at a distance of 4⅛ ins. from each other. Now draw a second outer circle of 22 ins. diameter. This indicates the depth of the scallop.

After preparing the lace start to pin out the cloth trying to shape the scallops according to photo. Put the two loops of 5 chain on to one pin only, placing it on to the mark of the inner circle, which gives the inner point of each scallop. The outer point of the scallop is obtained by pinning down the two central loops of chain in the middle of the scallop, separately, on to the outer circle. Then pin down the remaining loops of chain according to photo or to one's own liking.

Finish treating the lace as directed in the BASIC INSTRUCTIONS.

"Sun Ray" Design Dinner Cloth

"Sun Ray" Design

Afternoon Tea Cloth and Dinner Cloth

MATERIALS :—

TEA CLOTH—3 balls of Crochet Cotton No. 60.

DINNER CLOTH—9 balls of Crochet Cotton No. 60.

Four double pointed knitting needles No. 12, length 7 ins.

One circular knitting needle No. 12, length 24″, and one circular knitting needle No. 12, length 36″ or 42″.

One steel crochet hook No. 5.

MEASUREMENTS :—

TEA CLOTH—32 ins. diameter.

DINNER CLOTH—62 ins. diameter.

Afternoon Tea Cloth

When working the TEA CLOTH follow the instructions of CASTING-ON and PARTS A, B, C, and D as given for the DINNER CLOTH. Then knit according to directions of PART E 2. Proceed to FINISHING of TEA CLOTH.

Dinner Cloth

CASTING-ON :—

Commence by casting on 10 stitches (either method) having 3 stitches on the first, 3 stirches on the second, and 4 stitches on the third needle. Consequently 3 sections of one round of PART A will be knitted on each of the first two needles, and 4 sections on the third needle. Then knit one round plain and work first pattern round of PART A.

Every round of which the number is missing knit plain. Care should be taken of Yo. 2 as previously explained.

PART A.

Knit each section from [to] 10 times in one round.

1st round.—[Yo., K.1.]

3rd round.—[Yo., K.2 tog.]

4th round.—[M.3, K.1.]

Four rounds plain.

9th round.—[Yo., K.2 tog., Yo., K.2 tog.]

10th round.—[M.3, K.1, M.3, K.1.]

Six rounds plain.

Now proceed with PART B.

PART B.

Notice that all rounds up to 28 are pattern rounds.

Knit each section from [to] 20 times in one round.

17th round.—[K.1, Yo., K.2, Yo., K.1.]

18th round.—[K.1, M.2 (into Yo. of previous round), K.2, M.2, K.1.]

19th round.—[(K.2 tog., Yo., S1.1, K.1, psso.) twice]

20th round.—[K.1, M.2 (into Yo. of previous round), K.2, M.2, K.1.]

21st round.—same as 19th round.

22nd round.—same as 20th round.

23rd round.—same as 19th round.

24th round.—same as 20th round.

25th round.—same as 19th round.

26th round.—same as 20th round.

27th round.—same as 19th round.

28th round.—[K.1, M.5 (into Yo. of previous round), K.2, M.5, K.1.]

Two rounds plain.

31st round.—[Yo., S1.1, K.1, psso., K.10, K.2 tog.]

33rd round.—[Yo., K.1B., Yo., S1.1, K.1, psso., K.8, K.2 tog.]

35th round.—[K.1, Yo., K.1B., Yo., K.1, S1.1, K.1, psso., K.6, K.2 tog.]

37th round.—[K.2, Yo., K.1B., Yo., K.2, S1.1, K.1, psso., K.4, K.2 tog.]

39th round.—[K.3, Yo., K.1B., Yo., K.3, S1.1, K.1, psso., K.2, K.2 tog.]

41st round.—[K.4, Yo., K.1B., Yo., K.4, S1.2, K.2 tog., p2sso.]

43rd round.—[(K.5, Yo., K.1B., Yo.,) twice.]

45th round.—[S1.1, K.1, psso., K.9, K.2 tog., K.1, Yo., K.1B., Yo., K.1.]

47th round.—[S1.1, K.1. psso., K.7, K.2 tog., K.2, Yo., K.1B., Yo., K.2.]

49th round.—[S1.1, K.1, psso., K.5, K.2 tog., K.3, Yo., K.1B., Yo., K.3.]

51st round.—[S1.1, K.1, psso., K.3, K.2 tog., K.4, Yo., K.1B., Yo., K.4.]

53rd round.—[S1.1, K.1, psso., K.1, K.2 tog., K.5, Yo., K.1B., Yo., K.5.]

55th round.—[S1.1, K.2 tog., psso., K.6, Yo., K.1B., Yo., K.6.]

57th round.—[Yo., K.1B., Yo., S1.1, K.1, psso., K.11, K.2 tog.]

59th round.—[Yo., K.3, Yo., S1.1, K.1, psso., K.9, K.2 tog.]

61st round.—[Yo., K.1, Yo., S1.1, K.2 tog., psso., Yo., K.1, Yo., S1.1, K.1, psso., K.7, K.2 tog.]

63rd round.—[Yo., K.3, Yo., K.1B., Yo., K.3, Yo., S1.1, K.1, psso., K.5, K.2 tog.]

65th round.—[Yo., K.1, (Yo., S1.1, K.2 tog., psso.) 3 times, Yo., K.1, Yo., S1.1, K.1, psso., K.3, K.2 tog.]

67th round.—[(Yo., K.3, Yo., K.1B.) twice, Yo., K.3, Yo., S1.1, K.1, psso., K.1, K.2 tog.]

69th round.—[Yo., K.1, (Yo., S1.1, K.2 tog., psso.) 5 times, Yo., K.1, Yo., S1.1, K.2 tog., psso.]

Now proceed with PART C.

PART C.

Knit each section from [to] 80 times in one round.

71st round.—[K.3, Yo., K.1B., Yo.]

73rd round.—[(S1.1, K.2 tog., psso., Yo.) twice.]

75th round.—[Yo., K.1B., Yo., K.3.]

77th round.—[(Yo., S1.1, K.2 tog., psso.) twice.]

79th round.—same as 71st round.

81st round.—same as 73rd round.

83rd round.—same as 75th round.

85th round.—same as 77th round.

87th round.—same as 71st round.

89th round.—same as 73rd round.

91st round.—same as 75th round.

93rd round.—same as 77th round.

Now proceed with PART D.

Notice that the next round is a pattern round.

PART D.

Knit each section from [to] 40 times in one round.

94th round.—[(M.3 into Yo. of previous round, K.1) 4 times.]

Two rounds plain.

97th round.—[K.14, K.2 tog., Yo.]

99th round.—[S1.1, K.1, psso., K.11, K.2 tog., Yo., K.1B., Yo.]

101st round.—[S1.1, K.1, psso., K.9, K.2 tog., K.1, Yo., K.1B., Yo., K.1.]

103rd round.—[S1.1, K.1, psso., K.7, K.2 tog., K.2, Yo., K.1B., Yo., K.2.]

105th round.—[S1.1, K.1, psso., K.5, K.2 tog., K.3, Yo., K.1B., Yo., K.3.]

107th round.—[S1.1, K.1, psso., K.3, K.2 tog., K.4, Yo., K.1B., Yo., K.4.]

109th round.—[S1.1, K.1, psso., K.1, K.2 tog., K.5, Yo., K.1B., Yo., K.5.]

111th round.—[S1.1, K.2 tog., psso., K.6, Yo., K.1B., Yo., K.6.]

113th round.—[(Yo., K.1B., Yo., K.7,) twice.]

115th round.—[K.1, Yo., K.1B., Yo., K.1, S1.1, K.1, psso., K.13, K.2 tog.]

117th round.—[K.2, Yo., K.1B., Yo., K.2, S1.1, K.1, psso., K.11, K.2 tog.]

119th round.—[K.3, Yo., K.1B., Yo., K.3, S1.1, K.1, psso., K.9, K.2 tog.]

121st round.—[K.4, Yo., K.1B., Yo., K.4, S1.1, K 1, psso., K.7, K.2 tog.]

123rd round.—[K.5, Yo., K.1B., Yo., K.5, S1.1, K.1, psso., K.5, K.2 tog.]

125th round.—[K.6, Yo., K.1B., Yo., K.6, S1.1, K.1, psso., K.3, K.2 tog.]

127th round.—[K.7, Yo., K.1B., Yo., K.7, S1.1, K.1, psso., K.1, K.2 tog.]

129th round.—[K.8, Yo., K.1B., Yo., K.8, Yo., S1.1, K.2 tog., psso., Yo.]

For Tea Cloth of 32 ins. diameter work PART E2.

If working the Dinner Cloth proceed now with Parts E, F, and G.

PART E.

Knit each section from [to] 40 times in one round.

131st round.—[Yo., S1.1, K.1, psso., K.15, K.2 tog., Yo., K.3.]

133rd round.—[Yo., K.1, Yo., S1.1, K.1, psso., K.13, K.2 tog., Yo., K.1, Yo., S1.1, K.2 tog., psso.]

135th round.—[K.3, Yo., S1.1, K.1, psso., K.11, K.2 tog., Yo., K.3, Yo., K.1B., Yo.]

137th round.—[Yo., S1.1, K.2 tog., psso., Yo., K.1, Yo., S1.1, K.1, psso., K.9, K.2 tog., Yo., K.1, (Yo., S1.1, K.2 tog., psso.) twice.]

139th round.—[K.1, Yo., S1.1, K.1, psso., K.2, Yo., S1.1, K.1, psso., K.7, K.2 tog., Yo., K.2, K.2 tog., Yo., K.1, Yo., K.1B., Yo.]

141st round.—[K.2, Yo., S1.1, K.2 tog., psso., Yo., K.1, Yo., S1.1, K.1, psso., K.5, K.2 tog., Yo., K.1, Yo., S1.1, K.2 tog., psso., Yo., K.2, Yo., S1.1, K.2 tog., psso., Yo.]

143rd round.—[K.1, (K.2, Yo., S1.1, K.1, psso.) twice, K.3, (K.2 tog., Yo., K.2,) twice, K.1, Yo., S1.1, K.2 tog., psso., Yo.]

145th round.—[K.4, Yo., S1.1, K.2 tog., psso., Yo., K.1, Yo., S1.1, K.1, psso., K.1, K.2 tog., Yo., K.1, Yo., S1.1, K.2 tog., psso., Yo., K.4, Yo., S1.1, K.2 tog., psso., Yo.]

147th round.—[K.5, Yo., S1.1, K.1, psso., K.2, Yo., S1.1, K.2 tog., psso., Yo., K.2, K.2 tog., Yo., K.5, Yo., S1.1, K.2 tog., psso., Yo.]

149th round.—[Yo., K.6, (Yo., S1.1, K.2 tog., psso.) 3 times, Yo., K.6, Yo., K.3.]

151st round.—[Yo., K.1, Yo., K.7, Yo., S1.1, K.1, psso., K.1, K.2 tog., Yo., K.7, Yo., K.1, Yo., S1.1, K.2 tog., psso.]

153rd round.—[K.3, Yo., S1.1, K.1, psso., K.6, Yo., S1.1, K.2 tog., psso., Yo., K.6, K.2 tog., Yo., K.3, Yo., K.1B., Yo.]

155th round.—[Yo., S1.1, K.2 tog., psso., Yo., K.1, Yo., S1.1, K.1, psso., K.13, K.2 tog., Yo., K.1, (Yo., S1.1, K.2 tog.,) twice.]

157th round.—[K.1, Yo., S1.1, K.1, psso., K.2, Yo., S1.1, K.1, psso., K.11, K.2 tog., Yo., K.2, K.2 tog., Yo., K.1, Yo., K.1B., Yo.]

159th round.—[K.2, Yo., S1.1, K.2 tog., psso., Yo., K.1, Yo., S1.1, K.1, psso., K.9, K.2 tog., Yo., K.1, Yo., S1.1, K.2 tog., psso., Yo., K.2, Yo., S1.1, K.2 tog., psso., Yo.]

161st round.—[K.1, (K.2, Yo., S1.1, K.1, psso.,) twice, K.7, (K.2 tog., Yo., K.2,) twice, K.1, Yo., S1.1, K.2. tog., psso., Yo.]

163rd round.—[K.4, Yo., S1.1, K.2 tog., psso., Yo., K.1, Yo., S1.1, K.1, psso., K.5, K.2 tog., Yo., K.1, Yo., S1.1, K.2 tog., psso., Yo., K.4, Yo., S1.1, K.2 tog., psso., Yo.]

165th round.—[K.3, (K.2, Yo., S1.1, K.1, psso.) twice, K.3, (K.2 tog., Yo., K.2) twice, K.3, Yo., S1.1, K.2 tog., psso., Yo.]

167th round.—[K.6, Yo., S1.1, K.2 tog., psso., Yo., K.1, Yo., S1.1, K.1, psso., K.1, K.2 tog., Yo., K.1, Yo., S1.1, K.2 tog., psso., Yo., K.6, Yo., S1.1, K.2 tog., psso., Yo.]

169th round.—[K.7, Yo., S1.1, K.1, psso., K.2, Yo., S1.1, K.2 tog., psso., Yo., K.2, K.2 tog., Yo., K.7, Yo., S1.1, K.2 tog., psso., Yo.]

171st round.—[Yo., K.8, (Yo., S1.1, K.2 tog., psso.) 3 times, Yo., K.8, Yo., K.3.]

173rd round.—[Yo., K.1, Yo., K.9, Yo., S1.1, K.1, psso., K.1, K.2 tog., Yo., K.9, Yo., K.1, Yo., S1.1, K.2 tog., psso.]

175th round.—[K.3, Yo., S1.1, K.1, psso., K.8, Yo., S1.1, K.2 tog., psso., Yo., K.8, K.2 tog., Yo., K.3, Yo., K.1B., Yo.]

177th round.—[Yo., S1.1, K.2 tog., psso., Yo., K.1, Yo., S1.1, K.1, psso., K.17, K.2 tog., Yo., K.1, (Yo., S1.1, K.2 tog., psso.) twice.]

179th round.—[K.1, Yo., S1.1, K.1, psso., K.2, Yo., S1.1, K.1, psso., K.15, K.2 tog., Yo., K.2, K.2 tog., Yo., K.1, Yo., K.1B., Yo.]

181st round.—[K.2, Yo., S1.1, K.2 tog., psso., Yo., K.1, Yo., S1.1, K.1, psso., K.13, K.2 tog., Yo., K.1, Yo., S1.1, K.2 tog., psso., Yo., K.2, Yo., S1.1, K.2 tog., psso., Yo.]

183rd round.—[K.1, (K.2, Yo., S1.1, K.1, psso.) twice, K.11, (K.2 tog., Yo., K.2) twice, K.1, Yo., S1.1, K.2 tog., psso., Yo.]

185th round.—[K.4, Yo., S1.1, K.2 tog., psso., Yo., K.1, Yo., S1.1, K.1, psso., K.9, K.2 tog., Yo., K.1, Yo., S1.1, K.2 tog., psso., Yo., K.4, Yo., S1.1, K.2 tog., psso., Yo.]

187th round.—[K.3, (K.2, Yo., S1.1, K.1, psso.) twice, K.7, (K.2 tog., Yo., K.2) twice, K.3, Yo., S1.1, K.2 tog., psso., Yo.]

189th round.—[K.6, Yo., S1.1, K.2 tog., psso., Yo., K.1, Yo., S1.1, K.1, psso., K.5, K.2 tog., Yo., K.1, Yo., S1.1, K.2 tog., psso., Yo., K.6, Yo., S1.1, K.2 tog., psso., Yo].

191st round.—[K.5, (K.2, Yo., S1.1, K.1, psso.) twice, K.3, (K.2 tog., Yo., K.2) twice, K.5, Yo., S1.1, K.2 tog., psso., Yo.]

193rd round.—[K.8, Yo., S1.1, K.2 tog., psso., Yo., K.1, Yo., S1.1, K.1, psso., K.1, K.2, tog., Yo., K.1, Yo., S1.1, K.2 tog., psso., Yo., K.8, Yo., S1.1, K.2 tog., psso., Yo.]

195th round.—[K.9, Yo., S1.1, K.1, psso., K.2, Yo., S1.1, K.2 tog., psso., Yo., K.2, K.2 tog., Yo., K.9, Yo., S1.1, K.2 tog., psso., Yo.]

197th round.—[Yo., K.10, (Yo., S1.1, K.2 tog., psso.) 3 times, Yo., K.10, Yo., K.3.]

199th round.—[Yo., K.1, Yo., K.11, Yo., S1.1, K.1, psso., K.1, K.2 tog., Yo., K.11, Yo., K.1, Yo., S1.1, K.2 tog., psso.]

201st round.—[K.3, Yo., S1.1, K.1, psso., K.10, Yo., S1.1, K.2 tog., psso., Yo., K.10, K.2 tog., Yo., K.3, Yo., K.1B., Yo.]

203rd round.—[Yo., S1.1, K.2 tog., psso., Yo., K.1, Yo., S1.1, K.1, psso., K.21, K.2 tog., Yo., K.1, (Yo., S1.1, K.2, tog., psso.) twice.]

205th round.—[K.1, Yo., S1.1, K.1, psso., K.2, Yo., S1.1, K.1, psso., K.19, K.2 tog., Yo., K.2, K.2 tog., Yo., K.1, Yo., K.1B., Yo.]

207th round.—[K.2, Yo., S1.1, K.2 tog., psso., Yo., K.1, Yo., S1.1, K.1, psso., K.17, K.2 tog., Yo., K.1, Yo., S1.1, K.2 tog., psso., Yo., K.2, Yo., S1.1, K.2 tog., psso., Yo.,]

209th round.—[K.1, (K.2, Yo., S1.1, K.1, psso.) twice, K.15, (K.2 tog., Yo., K.2) twice, K.1, Yo., S1.1, K.2 tog., psso., Yo.]

211th round.—[K.4, Yo., S1.1, K.2 tog., psso., Yo., K.1, Yo., S1.1, K.1, psso., K.13, K.2 tog., Yo., K.1, Yo., S1.1, K.2 tog., psso., Yo., K.4, Yo., S1.1, K.2 tog., psso., Yo.]

213rd round.—[K.3, (K.2, Yo., S1.1, K.1, psso.) twice, K.11, (K.2 tog., Yo., K.2) twice, K.3, Yo., S1.1, K.2 tog., psso., Yo.]

215th round.—[K.6, Yo., S1.1, K.2 tog., psso., Yo., K.1, Yo., S1.1, K.1, psso., K.9, K.2 tog., Yo., K.1, Yo., S1.1, K.2 tog., psso., Yo., K.6, Yo., S1.1, K.2 tog., psso., Yo.]

217th round.—[K.5, (K.2, Yo., S1.1, K.1, psso.) twice, K.7, (K.2 tog., Yo., K.2) twice, K.5, Yo., S1.1, K.2 tog., psso., Yo.]

219th round.—[K.8, Yo., S1.1, K.2 tog., psso., Yo., K.1, Yo., S1.1, K.1, psso., K.5, K.2 tog., Yo., K.1, Yo., S1.1, K.2 tog., psso., Yo., K.8, Yo., S1.1, K.2 tog., psso., Yo.]

221st round.—[K.7, (K.2 tog., Yo., S1.1, K.1, psso.) twice, K.3, (K.2 tog., Yo., K.2) twice, K.7, Yo., S1.1, K.2 tog., psso., Yo.]

223rd round.—[K.10, Yo., S1.1, K.2 tog., psso., Yo., K.1, Yo., S1.1, K.1, psso., K.1, K.2 tog., Yo., K.1, Yo., S1.1, K.2 tog., psso., Yo., K.10, Yo., S1.1, K.2 tog., psso., Yo.]

"Sun Ray" Design
Afternoon Tea Cloth used as Table Centre

225th round. [K.11, Yo., S1.1, K.1, psso., K.2, Yo., S1.1, K.2 tog., psso., Yo., K.2, K.2 tog., Yo., K.11, Yo., S1.1, K.2 tog., psso., Yo.]

227th round.—[K.12, (Yo., S1.1, K.2 tog., psso.) 3 times, Yo., K.12, Yo., K.3, Yo.]

229th round.—[K.13, Yo., S1.1, K.1, psso., K.1, K.2 tog., Yo., K.13, Yo., K.1, Yo., S1.1, K.2 tog., psso., Yo., K.1, Yo.]

231st round.—[S1.1, K.1, psso., K.12, Yo., S1.1, K.2 tog., psso., Yo., K.12, K.2 tog., Yo., K.3, Yo., K.1B., Yo., K.3, Yo.]

233rd round.—[S1.1, K.1, psso., K.25, K.2 tog., Yo., K.1, (Yo., S1.1, K.2 tog., psso.) 3 times, Yo., K.1, Yo.]

235th round.—[S1.1, K.1, psso., K.23, K.2 tog., (Yo., K.3, Yo., K.1B.) twice, Yo., K.3, Yo.]

237th round.—[S1.1, K.1, psso., K.21, K.2 tog., Yo., K.1, (Yo., S1.1, K.2 tog., psso.) 5 times, Yo., K.1, Yo.]
Notice next round is pattern.

238th round.—[K.25, (M.3, K.1,) 6 times, K.1.]
Now proceed with PART F.

PART F.

Care should be taken of Yo.2 as explained in BASIC INSTRUCTIONS.

Knit each section from [to] 40 times in one round.

239th round.—[S1.1, K.1, psso., K.19, K.2 tog., Yo., K.2 tog., K.23, S1.1, K.1, psso., Yo.]

241st round.—[S1.1, K.1, psso., K.17, K.2 tog., Yo., K.2 tog., K.23, S1.1, K.1, psso., Yo.]

Continued page 76.

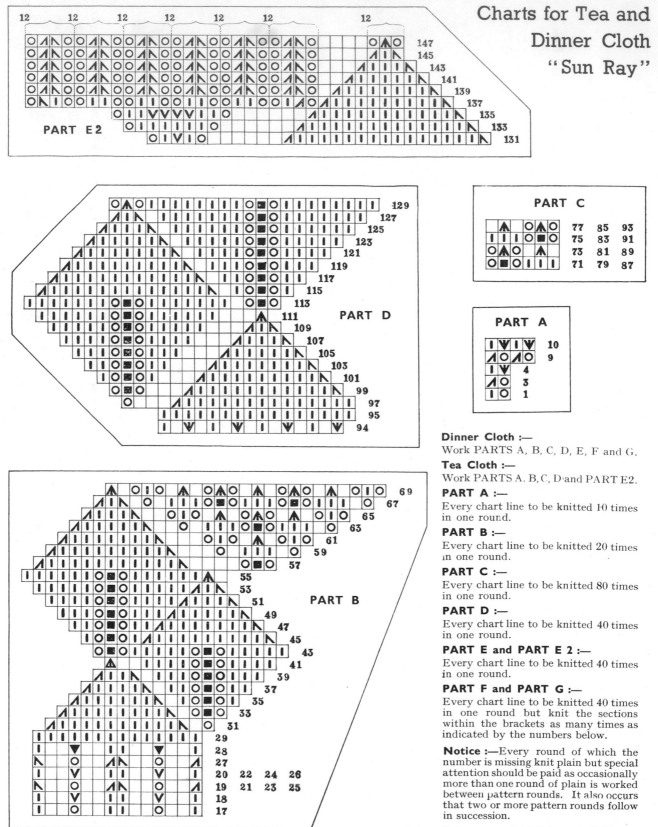

Dinner Cloth :—
Work PARTS A, B, C, D, E, F and G.

Tea Cloth :—
Work PARTS A, B, C, D and PART E2.

PART A :—
Every chart line to be knitted 10 times
in one round.

PART B :—
Every chart line to be knitted 20 times
in one round.

PART C :—
Every chart line to be knitted 80 times
in one round.

PART D :—
Every chart line to be knitted 40 times
in one round.

PART E and PART E 2 :—
Every chart line to be knitted 40 times
in one round.

PART F and PART G :—
Every chart line to be knitted 40 times
in one round but knit the sections
within the brackets as many times as
indicated by the numbers below.

Notice :—Every round of which the
number is missing knit plain but special
attention should be paid as occasionally
more than one round of plain is worked
between pattern rounds. It also occurs
that two or more pattern rounds follow
in succession.

Take care of M.5 in round 28.

74

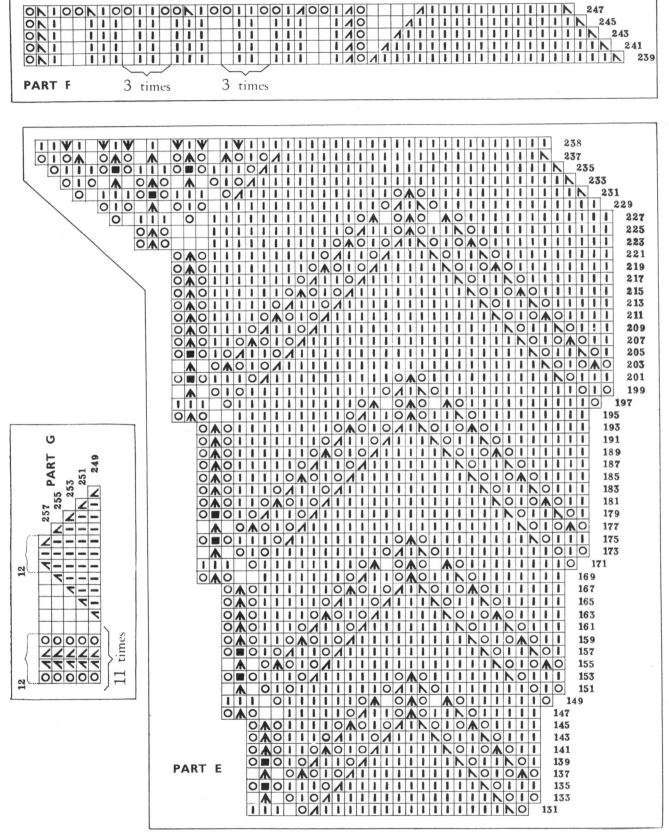

PART F   3 times   3 times

PART G

PART E

75

243rd round.—[S1.1, K.1, psso., K.15, K.2 tog., Yo., K.2 tog., K.23, S1.1, K.1, psso., Yo.]

245th round.—[S1.1, K.1, psso., K.13, K.2 tog., Yo., K.2 tog., K.23, S1.1, K.1, psso., Yo.]

247th round—[S1.1, K.1, psso., K.11, K.2 tog., (Yo., K.2 tog., K.1, Yo.) twice, (Yo., K.2, Yo.) 3 times, Yo., K.1, S1.1, K.1, psso., Yo., (Yo., K.2, Yo.) 3 times, (Yo., K.1, S1.1, K.1, psso., Yo.) twice.]

Now proceed with PART G.

PART G.

Knit each section from [to] 40 times in one round.

249th round.—[S1.1, K.1, psso., K.9, K.2 tog., (Yo., S1.1, K.1, psso., K.2 tog., Yo.) 11 times.]

251st round.—[S1.1, K.1, psso., K.7, K.2 tog., (Yo., S1.1, K.1, psso., K.2 tog., Yo.) 11 times.]

253rd round.—[S1.1, K.1, psso., K.5, K.2 tog., (Yo., S1.1, K.1, psso., K.2 tog., Yo.,) 11 times.]

255th round.—[S1.1, K.1, psso., K.3, K.2 tog., (Yo., S1.1, K.1, pssso., K.2 tog., Yo.) 11 times.]

257th round.—[S1.1, K.1, psso., K.1, K.2 tog., (Yo., S1.1, K.1, psso., K.2 tog., Yo.,) 11 times.]

258th round.—Knit plain.

See Finishing of DINNER CLOTH.

Afternoon Tea Cloth

PART E 2.

Care should be taken of Yo.2 as explained in BASIC INSTRUCTIONS.

Knit each section from [to] 40 times in one round.

131st round.—[S1.1, K.1, psso., K.15, K.2 tog., Yo., K.1, M.2, K.1, Yo.]

133rd round.—[S1.1, K.1, psso., K.13, K.2 tog., Yo., K.6, Yo.]

135th round.—[S1.1, K.1, psso., K.11, K.2 tog., Yo., K.2, (M.2,) 4 times, K.2, Yo.]

137th round.—[S1.1, K.1, psso., K.9, K.2 tog., Yo., K.2 tog., K.1, Yo., (Yo., K.2, Yo.,) 4 times, Yo., K.1, S1.1, K.1, psso., Yo.]

139th round.—[S1.1, K.1, psso., K.7, K.2 tog., (Yo., S1.1, K.1, psso., K.2, tog., Yo.) 6 times.]

141st round.—[S1.1, K.1, psso., K.5, K.2 tog., (Yo., S1.1, K.1, psso., K.2 tog., Yo.) 6 times.]

143rd round.—[S1.1, K.1, pssso., K.3, K.2 tog., (Yo., S1.1, K.1, psso., K.2 tog., Yo.) 6 times.]

145th round.—[S1.1, K.1, psso., K.1, K.2 tog., (Yo., S1.1, K.1, psso., K.2 tog., Yo.) 6 times.]

147th round.—[Yo., S1.1, K.2 tog., psso., Yo., (Yo., S1.1, K.1, psso., K.2 tog., Yo.) 6 times.]

148th round.—Knit plain.

See Finishing of TEA CLOTH.

FINISHING OF DINNER CLOTH.

After knitting plain round 258 finish the cloth by crocheting-off as follows :

3 sts., 1 d.c., 12 ch., (4 sts., 1 d.c., 12 ch.) 11 times. Repeat 39 times.

Finish with a slip stitch and break off. Secure thread invisibly.

FINISHING OF TEA CLOTH.

After knitting plain round 148 finish the cloth by crocheting-off as follows :

3 sts., 1 d.c., 12 ch., (4 sts., 1 d.c., 12 ch.) 6 times. Repeat 39 times.

Finish with a slip stitch and break off. Secure thread invisibly.

STRETCHING.

DINNER CLOTH

Prepare a paper pattern by drawing a circle of 60 ins. diameter. Mark round the circle 40 points at a distance of about 4¾ ins. from each other. Now draw a second outer circle of 62 ins. diameter. This indicates the depth of the scallop.

After preparing the lace, start to pin out the cloth trying to shape the scallops according to the photo, always pinning down two loops of chain with one pin only. First put the loops of chain on each side of the heavy point together on to one pin, placing it on to the mark of the inner circle, which gives the inner point of each scallop. The outer point of the scallop is obtained by pinning down the 2 central loops of chain in the middle of the scallop on to the outer circle. Then pin down the remaining loops of chain trying to shape the scallop into a pleasing form.

TEA CLOTH :—

Prepare a paper pattern by drawing a circle of 30 ins. diameter. Mark round the circle 40 points at a distance of about 2⅜ ins. from each other. Now draw a second outer circle of 32 ins. diameter. This indicates the depth of the scallop. After preparing the lace start to pin out the cloth, trying to shape the scallops according to photo. First put the loops of chain on each side of the heavy point together on to one pin only, placing it on to the mark of the inner circle, which gives the inner point of each scallop. The outer point of the scallop is obtained by pinning down the central loop of chain in the middle of the scallop on to the outer circle. Then pin down each remaining loop of chain with one pin only trying to shape the scallop in to a pleasing form.

Finish treating the lace pieces as directed in BASIC INSTRUCTIONS.

CHAPTER IV

WORKING INSTRUCTIONS
FOR SQUARE DESIGNS

"English Crystal" Design
Luncheon Set

"English Crystal" Design

Luncheon Set

MATERIALS:—

CENTRE PIECE, PLACE MAT, PLATE and GLASS MAT—2 balls of Crochet Cotton No. 40.

Four double pointed knitting needles No. 13. length 7 ins.
One steel crochet hook No. 4.

MEASUREMENTS:—

CENTRE PIECE.—13 ins. square.
PLACE MAT.—11 ins. square.
PLATE MAT.—9 ins. square.
GLASS MAT.—7 ins. square.

Centre Piece

CASTING-ON:—

Commence by casting on (either method) 8 stitches on to 3 needles having 2 stitches each on the first and second needle, and 4 stitches on the third needle. Work one round into the back of all stitches and knit first pattern round of PART A.

Every round of which the number is missing knit plain.

PART A.

Knit each section from [to] 4 times in one round.

1st round.—[Yo., K.1, Yo., K.1B.]

3rd round.—[Yo., K.3, Yo., K.1B.]

5th round.—[Yo., K.5, Yo., K.1B.]

7th round.—[Yo., K.7, Yo., K.1B.]

9th round.—[Yo., K.9, Yo., K.1B.]

11th round.—[Yo., K.11, Yo., K.1B.]

13th round.—[Yo., K.13, Yo., K.1B.]

15th round.—[Yo., Sl.1, K.1, psso., K.11, K.2 tog., Yo., K.1B.]

17th round.—[Yo., K.1, Yo., Sl.1, K.1, psso., K.9, K.2 tog., Yo., K.1, Yo., K.1B.]

19th round.—[Yo., K.3, Yo., Sl.1, K.1, psso., K.7, K.2 tog., Yo., K.3, Yo., K.1B.]

21st round.—[Yo., K.1, Yo., Sl.1, K.2 tog., psso., Yo., K.1, Yo., Sl.1, K.1, psso., K.5, K.2 tog., Yo., K.1, Yo., Sl.1, K.2 tog., psso., Yo., K.1, Yo., K.1B.]

23rd round.—[Yo., K.3, Yo., K.1B., Yo., K.3, Yo., Sl.1, K.1, psso., K.3, K.2 tog., (Yo., K.3, Yo., K.1B.) twice.]

Before knitting the following round pay special attention to the working of Yo.2 explained in BASIC INSTRUCTIONS.

25th round.—[Yo., K.1, (Yo.2, Sl.1, K.2 tog., psso.) 3 times, Yo.2, K.1, Yo., Sl.1, K.1, psso., K.1, K.2 tog., Yo., K.1, (Yo.2, Sl.1, K.2 tog., psso.) 3 times, Yo.2, K.1, Yo., K.1B.]

26th round.—Knit plain but take care to work 2 sts., i.e. (K.1, P.1) into Yo.2 of previous round. Proceed with PART B.

PART B.

Knit each section from [to] 4 times in one round.

Ignore asterisks when working PART B rounds 27 to 37 for the first time.

27th round.—[Yo., Sl.1, K.1, psso., K.5, * K.6, K.2 tog., Yo., Sl.1, K.2 tog., psso., Yo., Sl.1, K.1, psso., K.5, * K.6, K.2 tog., Yo., K.1B.]

29th round.—[Yo., K.1, Yo., Sl.1, K.1, psso., K.4, * K.5, K.2 tog., Yo., Sl.1, K.2 tog., psso., Yo., Sl.1, K.1, psso., K.4, * K.5, K.2 tog., Yo., K.1, Yo., K.1B.]

31st round.—[Yo., K.3, Yo., Sl.1, K.1, psso., K.3, * K.4, K.2 tog., Yo., K.3, Yo., Sl.1, K.1, psso., K.3, * K.4, K.2 tog., Yo., K.3, Yo., K.1B.]

33rd round.—[Yo., K.1, Yo., Sl.1, K.2 tog., psso., Yo., K.1, Yo., Sl.1, K.1, psso., K.2, * K.3, K.2 tog., Yo., K.1, Yo., Sl.1, K.2 tog., psso., Yo., K.1, Yo., Sl.1, K.1, psso., K.2, * K.3, K.2 tog., Yo., K.1, Yo., Sl.1, K.2 tog., psso., Yo., K.1, Yo., K.1B.]

35th round.—[Yo., K.3, Yo., K.1B., Yo., K.3, Yo., Sl.1, K.1, psso., K.1, * K.2, K.2 tog., Yo., K.3, Yo., K.1B., Yo., K.3, Yo., Sl.1, K.1, psso., K.1, * K.2, K.2 tog., (Yo., K.3, Yo., K.1B.) twice.]

Before knitting the following round pay again special attention to the working of Yo.2.

37th round.—[Yo., K.1, (Yo.2, Sl.1, K.2 tog., psso) 3 times, Yo.2, K.1, Yo., Sl.1, K.1, psso., * K.1, K.2 tog., Yo., K.1, (Yo.2, Sl.1, K.2 tog., psso.) 3 times, Yo.2, K.1, Yo., Sl.1, K.1, psso., * K.1, K.2 tog., Yo., K.1, (Yo.2, Sl.1, K.2 tog., psso.) 3 times, Yo.2, K.1, Yo., K.1B.]

38th round.—Knit plain but take care to work 2 sts., i.e. (K.1, P.1) into Yo.2 of previous round.

39th round to 50th round incl. are the same as rounds 27 to 38 but knit the part from * to * twice in each section.

51st round to 62nd round incl. are the same as rounds 27 to 38 but knit the part from * to * 3 times in each section.

Now see FINISHING OF LUNCHEON MATS.

Place Mat

Work according to instructions for CENTRE PIECE up to round 50 incl. and then see FINISHING OF LUNCHEON MATS.

Plate Mat

Work according to instructions for CENTRE PIECE up to round 38 incl. and then see FINISHING OF LUNCHEON MATS.

Glass Mat

Work according to instructions for CENTRE PIECE up to round 26 incl. and then see FINISHING OF LUNCHEON MATS.

FINISHING OF LUNCHEON MATS.

CENTRE PIECE.—After knitting last round knit one more stitch and then finish the lace mat with a chain of crochet as follows :

Work the section from [to] 4 times.

[2 sts., 1 d.c., 7 ch., (3 sts., 1 d.c., 7 ch.) 27 times, 2 sts., 1 d.c., 7 ch., 3 sts., 1 d.c., 7 ch.]

Finish with a slip stitch into first d.c. and break off.

PLACE MAT.—Crochet off as for CENTRE PIECE but work the part within the round brackets 21 times only.

PLATE MAT.—Crochet off as for CENTRE PIECE but work the part within the round brackets 15 times only.

GLASS MAT.—Crochet off as for CENTRE PIECE but work the part within the round brackets 9 times only.

STRETCHING OF LUNCHEON SET.

Prepare paper pattern for each of the four mats.

CENTRE PIECE.—Draw a square of 13 ins.

PLACE MAT.—Draw a square of 11 ins.

PLATE MAT.—Draw a square of 9 ins.

GLASS MAT.—Draw a square of 7 ins.

Now pin out the prepared mats by placing the corners into position first. All loops of chain are pinned out, with one pin only, at regular distances along the straight line.

Finish the lace by treating according to BASIC INSTRUCTIONS.

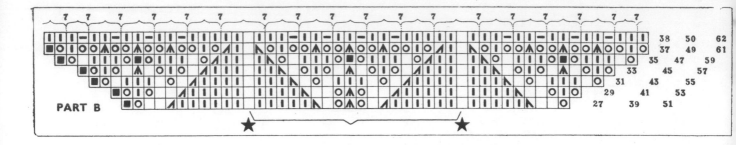

PART B

38 50 62
37 49 61
35 47 59
33 45 57
31 43 55
29 41 53
27 39 51

26
25
23
21
19
17
15
13
11
9
7
5
3
1

PART A

Charts for Luncheon Set "English Crystal"

Centre Piece:—
Work PARTS A and B up to round 62 incl.

Place Mat:—
Work PARTS A and B up to round 50 incl.

Plate Mat:—
Work PARTS A and B up to round 38 incl.

Glass Mat:—
Work PART A up to round 26.

PART A:—
Every chart line to be knitted 4 times in one round.

PART B:—
Every chart line to be knitted 4 times in one round but work the section from * to * as many times as PART B is repeated.

Every round of which the number is missing knit plain.

Pay special attention to the working of rounds 25 and 26, 37 and 38 etc.

Adaptation of "English Crystal" Design

The pattern of this design can easily be adapted to other measurements suitable for an Afternoon Tea-cloth or even a Dinner Cloth.

The casting-on and PART A remain the same always, measuring 5 ins. Then work PART B as many times as required, each repeat adds another 2 ins. to the lace cloth. When working PART B the repetition of the section from * to * will alter according to your adjustments.

It is perhaps advisable to knit one of the Luncheon Mats first, to get into the working of the pattern.

The photo on page 81 shows the adaptation of the " CRYSTAL " design to a cloth of 17 ins. square.

"Springtime" Design
Dinner Cloth

"Springtime" Design

Afternoon Tea Cloth and Dinner Cloth

MATERIALS :—

TEA CLOTH—4 balls of Crochet Cotton No. 60.
DINNER CLOTH—9 balls of Crochet Cotton No. 60.
Four double pointed knitting needles No. 12, length 7. ins.
One circular knitting needle No. 12, length 24 ins. and one circular knitting needle No. 12, length 36 ins.
One steel crochet hook No. 5.

MEASUREMENTS :—

TEA CLOTH—38 ins. square.
DINNER CLOTH—56 ins. square.
The design can be adapted to other measurements as given in ADAPTATION of PATTERN.

Dinner Cloth

Work according to directions given for TEA CLOTH. Cast on and knit PARTS A and B without alterations up to round 145 inclusive.

Then knit PART B rounds 27 to 49 inclusive another 4 times more which brings the rounds up to 241. With each repetition of PART B the repeat of the section from * to * also increases by the same number.

Having completed PART B for the last time proceed with working instructions of PART C the same as given for the TEA CLOTH, but notice, the section from * to * will be knitted 10 times. That brings the rounds up to 265.

Finally work PART D in which the section from * to * has to be knitted 11 times instead 7 times as stated for TEA CLOTH.

This will bring the rounds to 285. Round 286 knit plain and then see FINISHING of TEA AND DINNER CLOTH.

Afternoon Tea Cloth

CASTING-ON :—

Commence by casting on 8 stitches (either method) having 2 stitches on the first, 2 stitches on the second, and 4 stitches on the third needle. By help of this arrangement one quarter of a round will be worked on the first needle, one quarter on the second needle, and 2 quarters on the third needle. Now knit one round into the back of all stitches and then start to work the first pattern round of PART A.

Every round of which the number is missing knit plain.

PART A.

Knit each section from [to] 4 times in one round.

1st round.—[(Yo., K.1B.) twice.]

3rd round.—[Yo., K.3, Yo., K.1B.]

5th round.—[(Yo., K.2, Yo., K.1B.) twice.]

7th round.—[Yo., K.2 tog., M.3, K.1, Yo., K.1B., Yo., K.1, M.3, S1.1, K.1, psso., Yo., K.1B.]

9th round.—[(Yo., K.2 tog., K.1, M.3, K.1, S1.1, K.1, psso., Yo., K.1B.) twice.]

11th round.—[(Yo., K.2 tog., K.2, M.3, K.2, S1.1, K.1, psso., Yo., K.1B.) twice.]

13th round.—[(Yo., K.2 tog., K.3, M.3, K.3, S1.1, K.1, psso., Yo., K.1B.) twice.]

15th round.—[(Yo., K.2 tog., K.9, S1.1, K.1, psso., Yo., K.1B.) twice.]

17th round.—same as round 15.

19th round.—[Yo., K.2 tog., K.8, K.2 tog., Yo., K.3, Yo., S1.1, K.1, psso., K.8, S1.1, K.1, psso., Yo., K.1B.]

21st round.—[Yo., K.1, Yo., S1.1, K.1, psso., K.6, K.2 tog., Yo., K.5, Yo., S1.1, K.1, psso., K.6, K.2 tog., Yo., K.1, Yo., K.1B.]

23rd round.—[Yo., K.3, Yo., S1.1, K.1, psso., K.4, K.2 tog., Yo., K.7, Yo., S1.1, K.1, psso., K.4, K.2 tog., Yo., K.3, Yo., K.1B.]

25th round.—[Yo., K.1, Yo., S1.1, K.2 tog., psso., Yo., K.1, Yo., S1.1, K.1, psso., K.1, (K.1, K.2 tog., Yo., K.1, Yo., S1.1, K.1, psso., K.2) twice, K.2 tog., Yo., K.1, Yo., S1.1, K.2 tog., psso., Yo., K.1, Yo., K.1B.]

Now proceed with PART B.

PART B.

Knit each section from [to] 4 times in one round.

27th round.—[Yo., K.2, * K.1, Yo., S1.1, K.1, psso., K.2, Yo., S1.2, K.2 tog., p2sso., Yo., K.3, Yo., S1.1, K.1, psso., K.1, K.2 tog., Yo., K.3, Yo., S1.2, K.2 tog., p2sso., Yo., K.2, K.2, tog., Yo., K.2, * K.1, Yo., K.1B.]

29th round.—[Yo., K.2, Yo., K.1B., * Yo., K.2, (Yo., S1.1, K.2 tog., psso.) 3 times, Yo., K.1, Yo., S1.1, K.2 tog., psso., Yo., K.1, (Yo., S1.1, K.2 tog., psso.) 3 times, Yo., K.2, Yo., K.1B., * Yo., K.2, Yo., K.1B.]

31st round.—[Yo., K.2 tog., M.3, K.1, Yo., K.1B., * Yo., K.1, M.3, S1.1, K.1, psso., Yo., S1.1, K.1, psso., K.1, (K.1, Yo., K.1B., Yo., K.2) 3 times, K.2 tog., Yo., K.2 tog., M.3, K.1, Yo., K.1B., * Yo., K.1, M.3, S1.1, K.1, psso., Yo., K.1B.]

33rd round.—[Yo., K.2 tog., K.1, M.3, K.1, S1.1, K.1, psso., Yo., K.1B., * Yo., K.2 tog., K.1, M.3, K.1, S1.1, K.1. psso., Yo., (S1.1, K.2 tog., psso., Yo.) 7 times, K.2 tog., K.1, M.3, K.1, S1.1, K.1, psso., Yo., K.1B., * Yo., K.2 tog., K.1, M.3, K.1, S1.1, K.1 psso., Yo., K.1B.]

35th round.—[Yo., K.2 tog., K.2, M.3, K.2, S1.1, K.1, psso., Yo., K.1B., * Yo., K.2 tog., K.2, M.3, K.2, S1.1, K.1, psso., Yo., S1.1, K.1, psso., K.1, (K.1, Yo., K.1B., Yo., K.2,) twice, K.2 tog., Yo., K.2 tog., K.2, M.3, K.2, S1.1, K.1, psso., Yo., K.1B., * Yo., K.2 tog., K.2, M.3, K.2, S1.1, K.1, psso., Yo., K.1B.]

37th round.—[Yo., K.2 tog., K.3, M.3, K.3, S1.1, K.1, psso., Yo., K.1B., * Yo., K.2 tog., K.3, M.3, K.3, S1.1, K.1, psso., (Yo., S1.1, K.2 tog., psso.) 5 times, Yo., K.2 tog., K.3, M.3, K.3, S1.1, K.1, psso., Yo., K.1B., * Yo., K.2 tog., K.3, M.3, K.3, S1.1, K.1, pssso., Yo., K.1B.]

39th round.—[Yo., K.2 tog., K.9, S1.1, K.1, psso., Yo., K.1B., * Yo., K.2, tog., K.9, S1.1, K.1, psso., Yo., S1.1, K.1, psso., K.2, Yo., K.1B., Yo., K.2, K.2 tog., Yo., K.2 tog., K.9, S1.1, K.1, psso., Yo., K.1B., * Yo., K.2 tog., K.9, S1.1, K.1, psso., Yo., K.1B.]

41st round.—[Yo., K.2 tog., K.9, S1.1, K.1, psso., Yo., K.1B., * Yo., K.2 tog., K.9, S1.1, K.1, psso., (Yo., S1.1, K.2 tog., psso.,) 3 times, Yo., K.2 tog., K.9, S1.1, K.1, psso., Yo., K.1B., * Yo., K.2 tog., K.9, S1.1, K.1, psso., Yo., K.1B.]

43rd round.—[Yo., K.2 tog., K.8, K.2 tog., Yo., K.2, * K.1, Yo., S1.1, K.1, psso., K.8, S1.1, K.1, psso., Yo., S1.1, K.1, psso., K.1, K.2 tog., Yo., K.2 tog., K.8, K.2 tog., Yo., K.2, * K.1, Yo., S1.1, K.1, psso., K.8, S1.1, K.1, psso., Yo., K.1B.]

45th round.—[Yo., K.1, Yo., S1.1, K.1, psso., K.6, K.2 tog., Yo., K.3, * K.2, Yo., S1.1, K.1, psso., K.6, K.2 tog., Yo., K.1, Yo., S1.1, K.2 tog., psso., Yo., K.1, Yo., S1.1, K.1, psso., K.6, K.2 tog., Yo., K.3, * K.2, Yo., S1.1, K.1, psso., K.6, K.2 tog., Yo., K.1, Yo., K.1B.]

47th round.—[Yo., K.3, Yo., S1.1, K.1, psso., K.4, K.2 tog., Yo., K.4, * K.3, Yo., S1.1, K.1, psso., K.4, K.2 tog., Yo., K.3, Yo., K.1B., Yo., K.3, Yo., S1.1, K.1, psso., K.4, K.2 tog., Yo., K.4, * K.3, Yo., S1.1, K.1, psso., K.4, K.2 tog., Yo., K.3, Yo., K.1B.]

49th round.—[Yo,, K.1, Yo., S1.1, K.2 tog., psso., Yo., K.1, Yo., S1.1, K.1, psso., K.2, K.2 tog., Yo., K.1, Yo., S1.1, K.1, psso., K.2, * K.1, K.2 tog., Yo., K.1, Yo., S1.1, K.1, psso., K.2, K.2 tog., Yo., K.1, (Yo., S1.1, K.2 tog., psso.) 3 times, Yo., K.1, Yo., S1.1, K.1, psso., K.2, K.2 tog., Yo., K.1, Yo., S1.1, K.1, psso., K.2, * K.1, K.2 tog., Yo., K.1, Yo., S1.1, K.1, psso., K.2, K.2 tog., Yo., K.1, Yo., S1.1, K.2 tog., psso., Yo., K.1, Yo., K.1B.]

Rounds 51 up to 73 are the same as rounds 27 to 49 incl. but knit the part from * to * twice in every section.

Rounds 75 up to 97 are the same as rounds 27 to 49 incl. but knit the part from * to * 3 times in every section.

Rounds 99 up to 121 are the same as rounds 27 to 49 incl. but knit the part from * to * 4 times in every section.

Rounds 123 up to 145 are the same as rounds 27 to 49 incl. but knit the part from * to * 5 times in every section.

Now proceed with PARTC.

PART C.

Knit each section from [to] 4 times in one round.

147th round.—[Yo., K.3, * Yo., S1.1, K.1, psso., K.2, Yo., S1.2, K.2 tog., p2sso., Yo., K.3, Yo., S1.1, K.1, psso., K.1, K.2 tog., Yo., K.3, Yo., S1.2, K.2 tog., p2sso., Yo., K.2, K.2 tog., Yo., K.3, * rep. 5 times more from * to *, Yo., K.1B.]

149th round.—[Yo., K.1, Yo., S1.1, K.2 tog., psso., * Yo., K.1, (Yo., S1.1, K.2 tog., psso.) 3 times, Yo., K.1, Yo., S1.1, K.2 tog., psso., Yo., K.1, (Yo., S1.1, K.2 tog., psso.,) 3 times, Yo., K.1, Yo., S1.1, K.2 tog., psso., * rep. 5 times more * to * Yo., K.1, Yo., K.1B.]

151st round.—[Yo., K.3, Yo., K.1B., Yo., * K.3, Yo., S1.1, K.1, psso., (K.2, Yo., K.1B., Yo., K.1,) 3 times, K.1, K.2 tog., Yo., K.3, Yo., K.1B., Yo., * rep. 5 times more from * to *, K.3, Yo., K.1B.]

153rd round.—[Yo., K.1, (Yo., S1.1, K.2 tog., psso.) twice, Yo., * S1.1, K.2 tog., psso., Yo., K.1, (Yo., S1.1, K.2 tog., pssso.,) 7 times, Yo., K.1, (Yo., S1.1, K.2 tog., psso.) twice, Yo., * rep. 5 times more from * to *, S1.1, K.2 tog., psso., Yo., K.1, Yo., K.1B.]

155th round.—[Yo., K.3, Yo., K.1B., Yo., K.3, * Yo., K.1B., Yo., K.3, Yo., S1.1, K.1, psso., (K.2, Yo., K.1B., Yo., K.1) twice, K.1, K.2 tog., Yo., K.3, Yo., K.1B., Yo., K.3, * rep. 5 times more from * to *, Yo., K.1B., Yo., K.3, Yo., K.1B.]

157th round.—[Yo., K.1, (Yo., S1.1, K.2 tog., psso.) 3 times, * (Yo., S1.1, K.2 tog., psso.) twice, Yo., K.1, (Yo., S1.1, K.2 tog., psso.) 5 times, Yo., K.1, (Yo., S1.1, K.2 tog., psso.) 3 times, * rep. 5 times more from * to *, (Yo., S1.1, K.2 tog., psso.) twice, Yo., K.1, Yo., K.1B.]

159th round.—[Yo., (K.3, Yo., K.1B., Yo.) twice, * K.3, Yo., K.1B., Yo., K.3, Yo., S1.1, K.1, psso., K.2, Yo., K.1B., Yo., K.2, K.2 tog., (Yo., K.3, Yo., K.1B.) twice, Yo., * rep. 5 times more from * to *, K.3, Yo., K.1B., Yo., K.3, Yo., K.1B.]

161st round.—[Yo., K.1, Yo., (S1.1, K.2 tog., psso., Yo.,) 4 times, * (S1.1, K.2 tog., psso., Yo.) 3 times, K.1, (Yo., S1.1, K.2 tog., psso.) 3 times, Yo., K.1, Yo., (S1.1, K.2 tog., psso., Yo.) 4 times, * rep. 5 times more from * to *, (S1.1, K.2 tog., psso., Yo.) 3 times, K.1, Yo., K.1B.]

163rd round.—[Yo., K.3, (Yo., K.1B., Yo., K.3) twice, * (Yo., K.1B., Yo., K.3) twice, Yo., S1.1, K.1, psso., K.1, K.2 tog., Yo., K.3, (Yo., K.1B., Yo., K.3) twice * rep. 5 times more from * to * (Yo., K.1B., Yo., K.3) twice, Yo., K.1B.]

165th round.—[Yo., K.1, (Yo., S1.1, K.2 tog., psso.) 5 times, * (Yo., S1.1, K.2 tog., psso.) 4 times, Yo., K.1, Yo., S1.1, K.2 tog., psso., Yo., K.1, (Yo., S1.1, K.2 tog., psso.) 5 times, * rep. 5 times more from * to *, (Yo., S1.1, K.2 tog., psso.) 4 times, Yo., K.1, Yo., K.1B.]

167th round.—[Yo., (K.3, Yo., K.1B., Yo.) 3 times, * (K.3, Yo., K.1B., Yo.) 6 times, * rep. 5 times more from * to *, (K.3, Yo., K.1B., Yo.) twice, K.3, Yo., K.1B.]

169th round.—[Yo., K.1, Yo., (S1.1, K.2 tog., psso., Yo.) 6 times, * (S1.1, K.2 tog., psso., Yo.) 12 times, * rep. 5 times more from * to *, (S1.1, K.2 tog., psso., Yo.) 5 times, K.1, Yo., K.1B.]

Now proceed with PART D.

PART D.

Knit each section from [to] 4 times in one round.

171st round.—[Yo., K.2, * K.1, Yo., S1.1, K.1, psso., (K.2, Yo., K.1B., Yo., K.1) 4 times, K.1, K.2 tog., Yo., K.2, * rep. 6 times more from * to *, K.1, Yo., K.1B.]

173rd round.—[Yo., K.2, Yo., K.1B., * Yo., K.2, (Yo., S1.1, K.2 tog., psso.) 9 times, Yo., K.2, Yo., K.1B., * rep. 6 times more from * to *, Yo., K.2, Yo., K.1B.]

175th round.—[Yo., K.2 tog., M.3, K.1, Yo., K.1B., * Yo., K.1, M.3, S1.1, K.1, psso., Yo., S1.1, K.1, psso., (K.2, Yo., K.1B., Yo., K.1) 3 times, K.1, K.2 tog., Yo., K.2 tog., M.3, K.1, Yo., K.1B., * rep. 6 times more from * to *, Yo., K.1, M.3, S1.1, K.1, psso., Yo., K.1B.]

177th round.—[Yo., K.2 tog., K.1, M.3, K.1, S1.1, K.1, psso., Yo., K.1B., * Yo., K.2 tog., K.1, M.3, K.1, S1.1, K.1, psso., (Yo., S1.1, K.2 tog., psso.,) 7 times, Yo., K.2 tog., K.1, M.3, K.1, S1.1, K.1, psso., Yo., K.1B. * rep. 6 times more from * to *, Yo., K.2 tog., K.1, M.3, K.1, S1.1, K.1, psso., Yo., K.1B.]

179th round.—[Yo., K.2 tog., K.2, M.3, K.2, S1.1, K.1, psso., Yo., K.1B., * Yo., K.2 tog., K.2, M.3, K.2, S1.1, K.1, psso., Yo., S1.1, K.1, pssso., (K.2, Yo., K.1B., Yo., K.1) twice, K.1, K.2 tog., Yo., K.2 tog., K.2, M.3, K.2, S1.1, K.1, psso., Yo., K.1B., * rep. 6 times more from * to *, Yo., K.2 tog., K.2, M.3, K.2, S1.1, K.1, psso., Yo., K.1B.]

181st round.—[Yo., K.2 tog., K.3, M.3, K.3, S1.1, K.1, psso., Yo., K.1B., * Yo., K.2 tog., K.3, M.3, K.3, S1.1, K.1, psso., (Yo., S1.1, K.2 tog., psso.) 5 times, Yo., K.2 tog., K.3, M.3, K.3, S1.1, K.1, psso., Yo., K.1B., * rep. 6 times more from * to *, Yo., K.2 tog., K.3, M.3, K.3, S1.1, K.1, psso., Yo., K.1B.]

183rd round.—[Yo., K.2 tog., K.4, M.3, K.4, S1.1, K.1, psso., Yo., K.1B., * Yo., K.2 tog., K.4, M.3, K.4, S1.1, K.1, psso., Yo., S1.1, K.1, psso., K.2, Yo., K.1B., Yo., K.2, K.2 tog., Yo., K.2 tog., K.4, M.3, K.4, S1.1, K.1, psso., Yo., K.1B., * rep. 6 times more from * to *, Yo., K.2 tog., K.4, M.3, K.4, S1.1, K.1, psso., Yo., K.1B.]

185th round.—[Yo., K.2 tog., K.5, M.3, K.5, S1.1, K.1, psso., Yo., K.1B., * Yo., K.2 tog., K.5, M.3, K.5, S1.1, K.1, psso., (Yo., S1.1, K.2 tog., psso.) 3 times, Yo., K.2 tog., K.5, M.3, K.5, S1.1, K.1, psso., Yo., K.1B., * rep. 6 times more from * to *, Yo., K.2 tog., K.5, M.3, K.5, S1.1, K.1, psso., Yo., K.1B.]

187th round.—[Yo., K.2 tog., K.13, S1.1, K.1, psso., Yo., K.1B., * Yo., K.2 tog., K.13, S1.1, K.1, psso., Yo., S1.1, K.1, psso., K.1, K.2 tog., Yo., K.2 tog., K.13, S1.1, K.1, psso., Yo., K.1B., * rep. 6 times more from * to *, Yo., K.2 tog., K.13, S1.1, K.1, psso., Yo., K.1B.]

189th round.—[K.2 tog., K.13, S1.1, K.1, psso., Yo., K.1B., * Yo., K.2 tog., K.13, S1.1, K.1, psso., Yo., S1.1, K.2 tog., psso., Yo., K.2 tog., K.13, S1.1, K.1, psso., Yo., K.1B., * rep. 6 times more from * to *, Yo., K.2 tog., K.13, S1.1, K.1, psso., Yo., K.1B., Yo.]

190th round.—Knit plain.

Now see FINISHING of CLOTH.

FINISHING OF TEA AND DINNER CLOTH :—

After knitting last plain round finish the cloth with a chain of crochet as follows :

*(3 sts., 1 d.c., 9 ch.) 10 times, (3 sts., 1 d.c., 5 ch.) twice *. Work from * to * 32 times for TEA CLOTH, and 48 times for DINNER CLOTH. Finish with a slip stitch and break off. Secure thread invisibly.

STRETCHING :—

TEA CLOTH :

Prepare paper pattern by drawing a square of 36 ins. Divide each side of the square into 8 parts of 4½ ins. length, starting at the corner. Now draw a second outer square of 38 ins. This indicates the depth of the scallop.

DINNER CLOTH :

Prepare paper pattern by drawing a square of 54 ins. Divide each side of the square into 12 parts of 4½ ins. length, starting at the corner. Now draw a second outer square of 56 ins. This indicates the depth of the scallop. The following instructions apply to both sizes.

After preparing the lace start to pin out the cloth trying to shape the scallops according to the photo, pinning out the corners first.

Put the two loops of 5 chain on to one pin only, placing it on to the mark of the inner square which gives the inner point of each scallop. The outer point of the scallop is obtained by pinning down the two central loops of chain in the middle of the scallop, separately on to the outer square. Then pin down the remaining loops of chain in to a scallop taking always two loops on to one pin.

Finish treating the lace as directed in BASIC INSTRUCT-IONS.

Adaptation of "Springtime" Design

The pattern of the SPRINGTIME DESIGN can easily be adapted to various other measurements as given for TEA and DINNER CLOTH.

The casting on and PART A always remain the same and measure 4½ ins.

Then work PART B as many times as you require. Each repeat enlarges the cloth by another 4½ ins.

After having worked PART B the number of times wanted, knit PARTS C and D as given in pattern but the number of sections from * to * will have altered accordingly to your adjustments. PARTS C and D together add another 9 ins. to your measurements.

Charts for
Tea and Dinner Cloth
"Springtime"

TEA CLOTH:

Work PART A, PART B 5 times, PARTS C AND D.

DINNER CLOTH:

Work PART A, PART B 9 times, PARTS C and D.
Every round of which the number is missing knit plain.

PART A:—

Every chart line to be knitted 4 times in one round.

PART B:—

Every chart line to be knitted 4 times in one round but work the section within the bracket as many times as PART B is repeated. (e.g. When knitting PART B for the first time the section from * to * will be worked once. When knitting PART B the second time the section of every chart line within the bracket will be worked twice etc.)

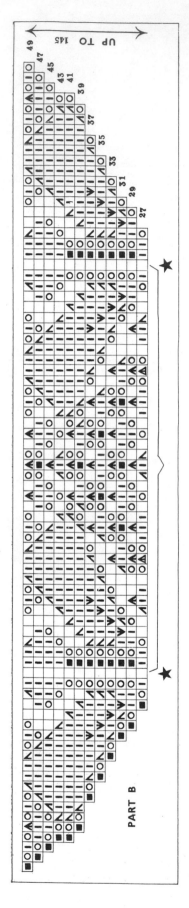

PART B

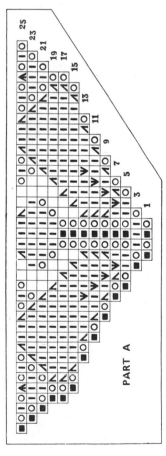

PART A

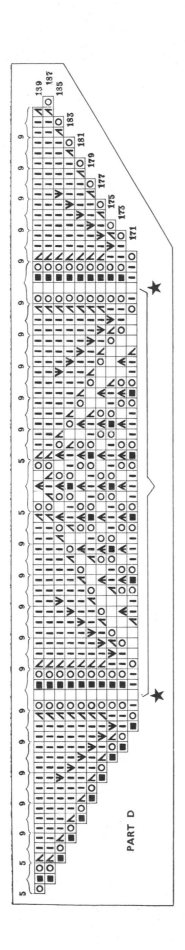

PART D

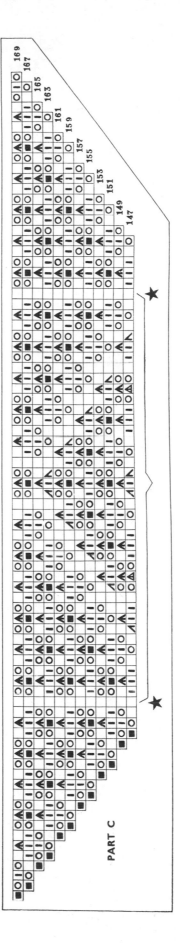

PART C

PART C :—

Every chart line to be knitted 4 times in one round but work the section within the bracket 6 times when knitting the TEA CLOTH and 10 times when knitting the DINNER CLOTH.

PART D :—

Every chart line to be knitted 4 times in one round but knit the section from * to * 7 times when working the TEA CLOTH and 11 times for the DINNER CLOTH.

"Three of Hearts" Design

Cushion Cover

MATERIALS:—

3 balls of Crochet Cotton No. 40.

4 double pointed knitting needles No. 12, length 9 ins., or one circular knitting needle No. 12, length 24 ins.

One steel crochet hook No. 4.

MEASUREMENTS:—

About 20 ins. square. Other measurements see ADAPTATION OF PATTERN.

CASTING-ON:—

Commence by casting on 288 stitches on to 3 needles having 96 stitches on each needle, or cast all stitches on to a 24 in. circular needle which will facilitate the work considerably. Knit one round plain and knit first pattern round of PART A.

Every round of which the number is missing knit plain.

PART A.

1st round.—(Yo., K.2 tog.) to be worked to the end of round.

7 rounds plain.

9th round.—as 1st round.

7 rounds plain.

17th round.—(Sl.1, K.2 tog., psso., Yo.) to be worked to the end of round.

19th round.—(Yo., K.1B., Yo., K.3) to be worked to the end of round.

21st round.—(Yo., Sl.1, K.2 tog., psso.) work to end of round.

23rd round.—(K.3, Yo., K.1B., Yo.) to end of round. Proceed with PART B.

PART B.

Knit each section from [to] 6 times in one round.

25th round.—(Sl.1, K.2 tog., psso., Yo.) to end of round.

27th round.—(Yo., K.1B., Yo., K.3) to end of round.

29th round.—[(Yo., Sl.1, K.2 tog., psso.) 4 times, Yo., K.1, M.2, K.1, (Yo., Sl.1, K.2 tog., psso.) 7 times, Yo., K.1, M.2, K.1, (Yo., Sl.1, K.2 tog., psso.) 3 times.]

31st round.—[K.3, Yo., K.1B., Yo., K.2, K.2 tog., Yo., K.6, Yo., Sl.1, K.1, psso., (K.2, Yo., K.1B., Yo., K.1) twice, K.1, K.2 tog., Yo., K.6, Yo., Sl.1, K.1, psso., K.2, Yo., K.1B., Yo.]

33rd round.—[(Sl.1, K.2 tog., psso., Yo.) 3 times, K.8, (Yo., Sl.1, K.2 tog., psso.) 5 times, Yo., K.8, Yo., (Sl.1, K.2 tog., psso., Yo.) twice.]

35th round.—[(Yo., K.1B., Yo., K.2, K.2 tog., Yo., K.10, Yo., Sl.1, K.1, psso., K.2) twice.]

37th round.—[(Yo., Sl.1, K.2 tog., psso.) twice, Yo., K.12, Yo., Sl.1, K.2 tog., psso., Yo., K.1, M.2, K.1, Yo., Sl.1, K.2 tog., psso., Yo., K.12, Yo., Sl.1, K.2 tog., psso.]

39th round.—[K.3, Yo., K.1B., Yo., K.14, Yo., K.2 tog., K.4, Sl.1, K.1, psso., Yo., K.14, Yo., K.1B., Yo.]

41st round.—[(Sl.1, K.2 tog., psso., Yo.) twice, Sl.1, K.1, psso., K.10, K.2 tog., Yo., K.8, Yo., Sl.1, K.1, psso., K.10, K.2 tog., Yo., Sl.1, K.2 tog., psso., Yo.]

43rd round.—[Yo., K.1B., Yo., K.3, (Yo., Sl.1, K.1, psso., K.2, K.2 tog.,) twice Yo., K.10, (Yo., Sl.1, K.1, psso., K.2, K.2 tog.) twice, Yo., K.3.]

45th round.—[(Yo., Sl.1, K.2 tog., psso.) twice, (Yo., K.1, Yo., Sl.2, K.2 tog., p2sso.) twice, Yo., K.12, (Yo., Sl.2, K.2 tog., p2sso., Yo., K.1) twice, Yo., Sl.1, K.2 tog., psso.]

47th round.—[(K.3, Yo., K.1B., Yo.) 3 times, K.14, (Yo., K.1B., Yo., K.3) twice, Yo., K.1B., Yo.]

49th round.—[(Sl.1, K.2 tog., psso., Yo.) 6 times, Sl.1, K.1, psso., K.10, K.2 tog., (Yo., Sl.1, K.2 tog., psso.) 5 times, Yo.]

51st round.—[(Yo., K.1B., Yo., K.3) 3 times, (Yo., Sl.1, K.1, psso., K.2, K.2 tog.) twice, (Yo., K.3, Yo., K.1B.) twice, Yo., K.3.]

53rd round.—[(Yo., Sl.1, K.2 tog., psso.) 6 times, (Yo., K.1, Yo., Sl.2, K.2 tog., p2sso.) twice, Yo., K.1, (Yo., Sl.1, K.2 tog., psso.) 5 times.]

55th round.—(K.3, Yo., K.1B., Yo.) to the end of round.

Now work PART B rounds 25 to 55 incl. another 4 times which brings the rounds up to 183. Then proceed with PART C.

PART C.

185th round.—(Sl.1, K.2 tog., psso., Yo.) to the end of round.

187th round.—(Yo., K.1B., Yo., K.3) to the end of round.

189th round.—(Yo., Sl.1, K.2 tog., psso.) to the end of round.

Notice that next round is a pattern round.

190th round.—(M.2 into Yo. of previous round, K.1) to the end of round.

6 rounds plain.

197th round.—(Yo., K.2 tog.) to the end of round.

7 rounds plain.

205th round.—(Yo., K.2 tog.) to the end of round.

206th round.—Knit plain.

"Three of Hearts" Design

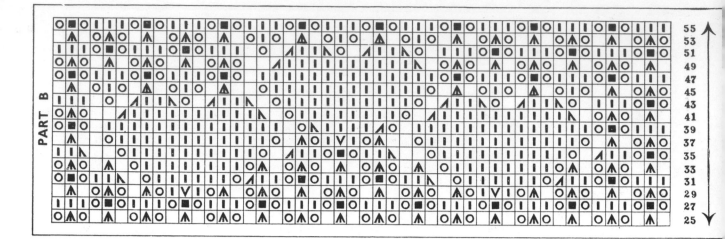

Charts for Cushion Cover
"Three of Hearts"

Work PART A, PART B 5 times, and then PART C.

PART A and PART C:—
Every chart line to be knitted 48 times in one round.

PART B:—
Every chart line to be knitted 6 times in one round.
Every round of which the number is missing knit plain.

FINISHING OF CUSHION COVER
After last plain round cast off rather loosely. Then place the cover in position, matching the pattern on both sides and stitch together the top edge, using the little holes as a guide. It is also possible to close the top edge with a row of Open Crochet, by joining the corresponding holes of the open row with 3 ch. making one d.c. alternately into the front and back row.

STRETCHING
Use fairly thick starch for final rinse and then stretch the Cushion-cover nicely into shape placing it on to a clean sheet etc. When almost dry press carefully pulling the lace at the same time to its correct measurements.

Adaptation of Design

The Cushion-cover can easily be enlarged by adding **96** sts. to the number given in the pattern. This will increase the width by about **6** ins.

The measurement of the depth of the Cushion is governed by PART B, each repetition adding about 3½ ins. to the size.